No. 674
$6.95

Professional Picture Framing for the Amateur

by Jack & Barbara Wolf

TAB BOOKS
Blue Ridge Summit, Pa. 17214

FIRST EDITION

FIRST PRINTING—APRIL 1974
SECOND PRINTING—NOVEMBER 1976

Hardbound Edition: International Standard Book No. 0-8306-3674-9

Paperbound Edition: International Standard Book No. 0-8306-2674-3

Library of Congress Card Number: 73-86764

Cover Photo: Courtesy National Paint and Coatings Association

PREFACE

This book, put together from our own practical experiences as owner-operators (until retirement) of a successful art gallery and framing business, provides the interested amateur framer or hobbyist with concise techniques to cover a wide spectrum of picture framing.

We call it **Professional Picture Framing for the Amateur** because that is exactly what it is. By following the methods outlined in the book, anyone with basic tools and materials and little or no practice can turn out not just a picture frame but a **professional** job.

We studied other "How to" books, and listened to comments from people who have used them, or tried to, and have made every effort to insure that our book is simple, direct, and really useful. It covers a full range of framing oils, pastels, watercolors, and other works under glass. Alternatives to the traditional rectangular molding frames are also discussed.

This book is a **practical** guide to picture framing. The accent is on the practical aspect, the production of good frames by methods readily applicable by even the most inexperienced beginner using tools which are available to all.

Rather than go into great detail about making up mouldings from lumber strips or builder's mouldings, processes which are hardly practical for even the most willing framer, we have indicated ways in which this may be done, but assumed that you the framer will most probably buy ready-cut mouldings for your use. (Anyone who has had experience at a lumber yard trying to find even two strips of wood which are sufficiently well cut and without warp and twist so that they might be joined as frame moulding needs to be joined will appreciate the nearly impossible task of trying to find four or five pieces to combine into an involved moulding. For the beginner, especially, this is something more readily done in theory than in practice.)

Involved and professional finishing is likewise avoided almost entirely. The person interested in making his own frames is seldom at a stage of professionalism to be building wire and plaster of paris or gypsum (gesso) armatures for creating the ornate Barbizon style frame any more than he is in learning the rather tricky techniques of metal leafing and tone finishing. The framers who are interested in this and who would be doing it are generally those already very skilled in the craft of framing and are doing restoration work or specialized custom framing. They are hardly in need of further instruction except perhaps in some highly specialized areas.

This book sets forth simple procedures for stain finishes and paint finishes which are easily within the technical range of the nonprofessional, and some additional direction is given for more involved finishes. The problems of the beginner or nonprofessional framer are seldom in the areas of advanced finishing. Few reach this point because they have no need for it. The nonprofessional framer is interested in making frames for his own work if he is an artist or, if indulging more as a hobbyist, for frames around someone else's work.

The approach in this book is to provide professional framing techniques simplified for your use. The main consideration has been to anticipate the many difficulties which you, the nonprofessional, will come across so that you can build attractive, successful frames as you need them. The problems in framing are seldom in the broad areas of building mouldings or in achieving Barbizon effects. Rather, the problems are in the small but vital processes of making a good joint, getting squared, flat frames, and having the parts properly fitted when final assembly is over. A well ma e frame, no matter how simple, is far more complimentary to a work of art than the most ornate frame poorly made.

The illustrations in this book were sketched by us and are, for the most part, greatly simplified. On the other hand, several of the diagrams have been significantly exaggerated simply to illustrate what should or should not happen in the given situation.

Good framing is a challenge. Practice and experience are the only substitutes for experience and practice, but first you must make a beginning: **this book!**

Jack and Barbara Wolf

CONTENTS

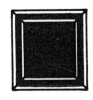

SECTION A
THE FRAME ITSELF

Tools for Framing

Since the object of this book is to provide a simplified approach to framing, all materials will be kept as simple as possible, including the tools needed. As you, the framer, become more experienced and adept at framing, you may decide to acquire tools and devices enabling you to do more complicated framing or faster work. There are many tools on the market for the professional framer or for the framer interested in 'production' framing, i.e., large-scale production. None of these are necessary for the beginner or occasional framer, no matter how skilled, and hence do not justify the expenditure. For the hobbyist more interested in the tools than in the product, it might well be another matter.

Throughout the book, mention will be made of some of the tools used by, or at least available to, the professional. The only purpose in doing this is to give you a broader idea of what is to be found and to inform you of some of the **potentials** in the field of framing. Many excellent professionals use even fewer or different tools than those listed here. Certainly, personal preference in framing, as in any craft, determines to a large extent the tools selected. The chapter on tools at the beginning of each section merely lists the tools needed to follow the processes described in the book. This is not dogma. Other tools may be used in addition, some of the tools may be substituted or left out, all depending on what you can accomplish with what is at hand. None of the tools listed are superfluous, however.

The basic steps in making the frame consist of **cutting** and of **joining.** The tools for cutting the necessary 45 degree (deg) angle end cuts are the chopper, the bench saw, and the backsaw and miter box. There are other specialized 'framing saws' which are modifications of the bench saw.

In A of the first illustration, we show the chopper, a foot- or motor-operated machine with cutting blades at right angles so that two miter cuts are made simultaneously when the cutting

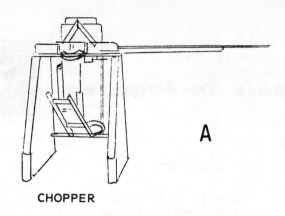

A

CHOPPER

head is lowered. The machine has a marked or calibrated bed so that exact lengths may be cut quickly and accurately. The name derives from the fact the cutting is done with a chopping action, as with a very sharp axe. This is an excellent machine and is fine for production work, as it cuts swiftly and makes two cuts in each operation, both a left- and a right-hand miter. They are not adaptable for any other cutting use, however, which is a serious disadvantage to the nonproduction or nonprofessional framer, and they are expensive compared to a good 10-inch bench saw. There are other minor disadvantages, but, since the chopper is NOT recommended except for the full-time professional, there is no point in discussing them.

MITER BOX AND
BACKSAW

B

The other basic cutting device is the saw. This may be either of the motor-driven type or the handsaw. If the handsaw is used, it should be of the backsaw type, a reinforced square blade which will not whip nor vibrate when being used. The common crosscut type handsaw is too flexible for use in framing. The backsaw should have at least 12 teeth per inch to make a clean cut and, for finer mouldings, closer to 20 teeth. It should also be long enough to allow your arm to move in long strokes. The construction-type backsaw and miter box are not really accurate nor fine enough for framing though they may be used in emergency.

The miter box, a device for assuring the 45 deg angle required in making rectangular frames, is shown in B, with a backsaw in place. This is merely a two- or three-sided wooden jig precut at 45 deg angles for right- and left-hand cuts. Because of its greater stability and guidance provided for the saw, the three-sided miter box is recommended for framing work. The two-sided should not be used.

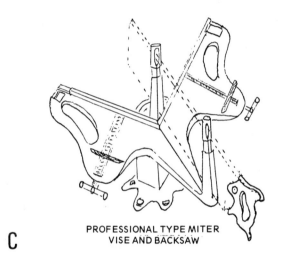

PROFESSIONAL TYPE MITER
VISE AND BACKSAW

C

A professional version of the same combination is shown in C. This is the factory-cast and -assembled miter and vise combination. The vise is one of the very best for joining, and the saw, held in place by sliding vertical guides, is very accurate. It cannot be used for anything but miter cutting, and it is hand-operated. Hand power is a disadvantage if much moulding is to be cut or if the moulding is of large, hard wood. A bench saw is not much more expensive and is more versatile as well as being less strenuous. You are cautioned, moreover,

11

that it is not good economy to purchase too cheap a miter box and saw if it is going to be used. A few dollars more for a good box, but especially for the better-quality saw, will be more than repaid later through the savings in joining and finishing the frame, as well as in labor.

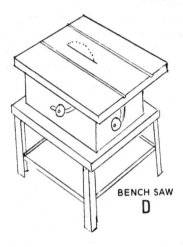

BENCH SAW
D

The most versatile cutter is, of course, the bench saw, and it is in general use by amateur and professional alike. A simplified version is shown in D. Professionals use the saw with either a 14- or 12-inch blade, but a 10-inch blade is usually enough for the serious beginner. The smaller amateur or hobbyist saws (with 8- or 9-inch blades) are usable but not recommended. In any case, the blade should have a cutting depth of at least 3½ inches for the higher mouldings. As we shall see later, if the miter jig is used, the effective cutting height is reduced by ¾ inch.

It should be mentioned in passing that a bandsaw is not recommended for framing work for a number of reasons. As for the newer radial-arm saws, there is no reason why they should not be adaptable for framing work as easily as the bench saw. The major points to check before use would be the possibility of vibration of the radial arm, and the accuracy of setting. If you are familiar with this type of saw, you will need no further discussion. If not familiar with it, discuss it thoroughly with the retailer at your hardware store.

There was at one time objection to the bench saw on the ground that it would not cut fabric-covered mouldings or liners as cleanly as would the chopper. With the improved clean-cut blades now available, the bench saw will cut as cleanly through the fabric as will any device on the market.

The blade is obviously a major concern when the bench saw is being used, no matter what model saw it may be. Note also that a high-speed motor is desirable, something in the range of 3800 revolutions per minute being standard. There are many types of blade available for the bench saw, each more or less developed for a specific purpose. There is also a general utility blade.

You should keep in mind that advantages in one sphere often create disadvantages in another. For example, a very fine-toothed blade for cabinet work may give very smooth cuts but not wear so long as would a coarser blade. This means replacement or resharpening before further use. Resharpened blades are never as good as factory-new ones, and usually they are definitely inferior to the point where they will splinter the mouldings. With fine mouldings, this can prove more expensive than the cost of new blades. Many professional shops have their blades sharpened each week as a matter of course. This is roughly based on the amount of moulding cut per week and, though sharpening may be cheaper for the production framer, you will probably not cut an equivalent amount in 2 years and would be better off to replace dull blades with new ones.

There are two blades on the market which best meet the demands of the framer. The first is the carbide-toothed blade and the other is the smooth-cut, hollow-ground blade.

The carbide blade is expensive in outlay though it justifies its cost if much cutting is to be done. Current carbide blades cost about $1.50 **per tooth**, when bought through the large dealers. A 10-inch blade for framing should have at least 48 teeth and preferably 72. This $1.50 per tooth is beyond the budget limitations of the average nonprofessional and, though it will cut about 15-20 times as much as the conventional blade before dulling, it is still more for the production framer than the occasional worker. With the carbide blade, it definitely pays to have a good resharpening job done when it dulls, and sending it back to the factory or to the factory-recommended sharpener is recommended. A poorly sharpened carbide blade will splinter mouldings to an unbelievable degree. The carbide blade also has a tendency to chip if it is used to cut nails or other hard materials unless it is one designed for this. Such a blade should be treated with care, a needless admonishment for those used to working with good tools.

Cheaper by far and most practical for the occasional framer is the smooth-cut, hollow-ground blade. This is a good utility blade for all types of moulding, and it cuts fabric covers and composition bases cleanly, provided it is **sharp**. The cut is so smooth that sanding before joining is unnecessary, a great advantage as we shall see later when discussing the joining of moulding. Blades of this type are available for under $10 for the 10-inch blade, and you can afford to replace them when they are dull—a blade will last for a very long time, if it is properly cared for. If you're doing a lot of cutting, it will still be economical to replace the blade when it dulls.

The bench saw has the additional advantage of being adaptable for cutting plywood backgounds, odd panels, and other work desired in framing, including cutting metals. There are special blades for nonferrous metals as there are for nails and work with ferrous metals, and you will have to decide on the right blade for the job. It is preferable to restrict the work done to a range requiring the minimum number of blades and, since most work may be done with two types of blades quite easily, this should present no problem.

Few framers will be cutting metals. Only in rare cases would such a blade be needed. As for the rough cutting of plywood and planking, a utility blade or a blade with as few as eight carbide teeth will suffice. An eight-tooth carbide blade of 10-inch diameter may be bought for around $12. This is excellent for coarser work and will last a long time. The other blade should be the smooth-cut, hollow-ground type for fine work and it should **never** be used for cutting plywood, Masonite or similar materials, especially those with glue binders.

BEWARE!—hand-held power saws of the circular or sabre type are completely unsuitable for framing.

For a bench saw, you'll need a set of two miter guides. One of these will be set at 45 deg for cutting off the right-hand end of the moulding stick, and the other used for the miter jig for cutting off the left hand end. The latter will be permanently mounted to the miter jig (as discussed in Chapter 3, explaining how to make the miter jig). The miter jig, and its positioning on the saw bench, is shown in E. The saw bench has grooves parallel to the saw blade to accommodate these miter guides.

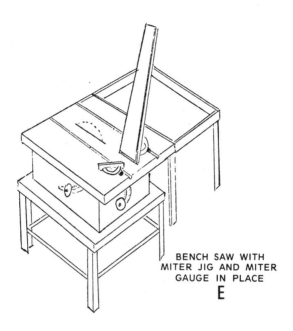

BENCH SAW WITH
MITER JIG AND MITER
GAUGE IN PLACE
E

The corner clamps which are recommended are shown in F. There are several types available, the better ones being those which are engineered as indicated in the diagram so that the tension screw pushes the movable jaw facing against the outer side of the moulding. Framers using the Stanley-Marsh or similar miter-vise and saw arrangements will have an excellent vise or clamp at hand. Such a vise without the saw and mitering component is also available.

The woodworker's vise is also used by some framers, especially those who use the single-clamp system of joining as we shall discuss in the chapter on joining. Even a metal-working vise is usable if the jaws are covered with cardboard or some such substance to protect the moulding, and if the pressure is applied carefully. In general, the type of miter clamp shown is recommended, and in sets of four, as the system preferred and outlined in this book is the four-clamp system. These small corner clamps are inexpensive, available for $2 or less each, and the investment is very small compared to the results.

Some professionals mount strong miter clamps on rounded wooden blocks, the better to compensate for faulty mouldings by being able to roll or twist the clamps while joining. This will not concern the nonprofessional or hobbyist.

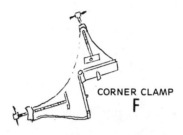

CORNER CLAMP
F

A quarter-inch hand drill is an absolute must for any framer. No matter how careful you may be, you simply cannot nail joints without splitting the moulding or chipping finish unless first drilling for the nails. Since various size nails and screws will be used, a selection of drill bits is also required. These should be complete from 1/16th to ¼ inch with a countersink for screw heads. Buy additional 1/16-inch bits, as these will be the most used and may break from time to time. The drill is also invaluable for predrilling for screw eyes and for other tasks to be discussed later.

Glue is indispensable in framing. There are some framers who claim that epoxy glues, without nailing, are absolutely strong and permanent. We prefer and recommend **nailing**, no matter what glue is used. The mechanical bond of the nail is cheap insurance and should be dispensed with only if the corners are held by some equally effective pinning action such as keyed joint or doweling. The latter are, however, techniques which are no longer much in use even by professionals. Ready-made frames are often held at the joints by metal lugs or by hidden staples, both forced into the wood under pressure in special machines. The nonproduction framer need not be concerned with such systems. As for glue itself, one of the most satisfactory is the common household white plastic glue obtainable in hardware and stationery stores. It is easy to apply, requires no special preparation, and

16

sets with a waterproof yet slightly flexible bond which has proven adequate for any framing. Unlike many of the special 'wood glues,' it does not dry out and turn brittle. It is also excellent, whether used diluted or full strength, for a wide range of other uses desired by the framer, such as mounting fabrics to backgrounds, gluing mats, and wetmounting (discussted later). The standard glue for woodworkers and framers was traditionally the casein glue which had to be used hot, but there is less used today.

In addition to the above, you should have an assortment of finishing nails and brads on hand. The most useful sizes are ¾ inch No. 20; 1 inch No. 19 or No. 20; and 1¼ inch No. 18. The types of moulding used will determine if these or other sizes are preferable. The same is true for screw eyes and wire, though Nos. 216½, 214½, and 211½ should take care of most framing needs. As for wire, a selection of 1, 3, and 5 gage should be adequate for most needs.

A good tack hammer, a fairly heavy carpenter's hammer, an accurate carpenter's try square, screwdrivers, and countersink for screw heads, are required. Sandpaper in several grades from very fine to coarse (000 to 2) should be readily available as should a good pair of scissors for cutting any fabrics desired in covering liners or backgrounds.

If some hand carving of the raw mouldings is contemplated, wood chisels and gouges will be needed, as will wood rasps. Some angle braces, of the type discussed later in the book, may be useful. A muffin tin is very handy for keeping various brads and screw eyes handy for use.

For touching up the moulding and filling in nail holes, there are numerous nail hole fillers in assorted colors available at most hardware stores. One of the easiest materials for this is the type which comes in sticks of assorted colors for retouching plywood paneling and other finished woods. The other tools needed for later stages in framing will be discussed at the beginning of each appropriate section.

2   *Cutting and Joining*

A picture frame utilizes the weakest type of joint in wood working—the end-to-end joint. For this reason, take care to insure that it is made no weaker by careless or inaccurate workmanship.

Round, oval, and hexagonal frames are not uncommon, but these and the semicircular fan frames are factory-made. For now, we will confine discussion to the rectangular frames most commonly in use.

This four-sided, four-cornered frame has four right angles. A right angle is one which subtends an arc of 90 deg. The miter cut on each end of the moulding must be 45 deg, as illustrated below.

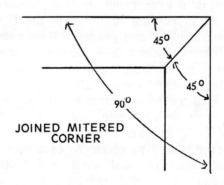

JOINED MITERED
CORNER

RABBET   LID

MITERED   LENGTH
OF   MOULDING

This angular measurement is absolutely exact and must be kept so. Any deviation will increase or decrease the corner angle and result in a frame which is not squared. The next illustration below, deliberately exaggerated, shows a frame which, if measured from end to end or side to side, would **seem** square. If checked with the try square, however, it would obviously be out of square.

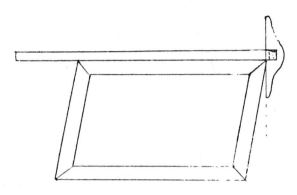

This can be prevented by making certain the miter cuts are accurate and, if four clamps are used, by keeping the frame in the clamps until the glue has set. Such off-square shifting of the frame can also be caused by slight warping in the moulding. Warping, etc., will be discussed in the chapter dealing with mouldings and their defects.

The need for accuracy is one of the reasons why a miter-box-backsaw combination is not satisfactory for serious framing unless it is of very good quality, such as mentioned before. Most miter boxes allow the saw to wobble or tilt, as shown in the series of illustrations following, with the resulting joining problems shown in the accompanying diagrams.

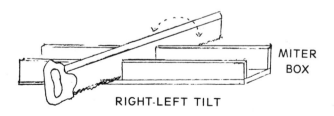

MITER BOX

RIGHT-LEFT TILT

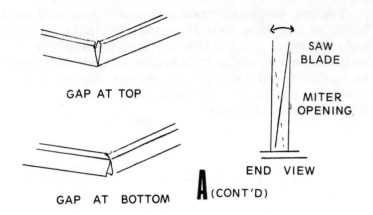

GAP AT TOP

SAW BLADE

GAP AT BOTTOM

MITER OPENING

END VIEW

A (CONT'D)

The same problems as in A above will occur in the use of the bench saw if the blade is not absolutely vertical to the bed. The situation shown in B does not occur on the bench saw, but there is an effect known as **creeping** which produces a deviation in the accuracy of the cut. This is caused by a tendency of the cut material to move into the saw blade, due to the

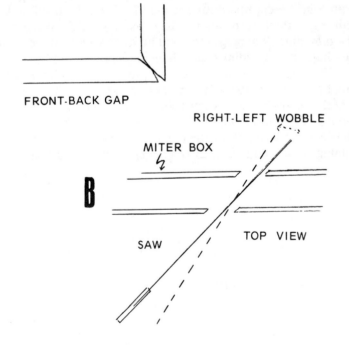

FRONT-BACK GAP

RIGHT-LEFT WOBBLE

MITER BOX

B

SAW

TOP VIEW

set of teeth or to the hollow grind of the blade. The result is an angle of more than 45 deg so that the frame when finished will have gaps to the outside of the frame as shown in A below. Creeping in the opposite direction would result in gaps as in B.

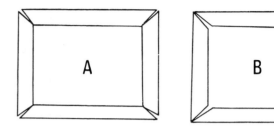

This creeping can be eliminated by soldering small points to the miter guide arm or the bed of the jig to penetrate into the base of the moulding ⅛ inch or so, as shown in the dotted lines on the diagram below, or by fixing a rough surface such as the metal scraper type from a grater or plasterer's metal finishing pad. Sandpaper can be glued on also, but this is less

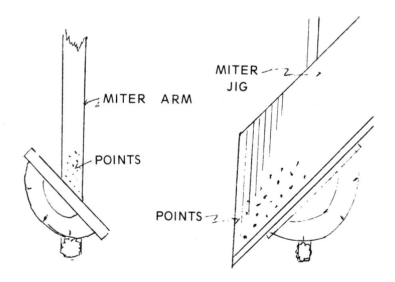

satisfactory as the moulding must be held immovable and the sandpaper stripping is not dependable. Nails may be driven into a miter box to prevent creeping, though this is not usually necessary.

All of the previous defects except the rounding of the cut can be caused by warped moulding and may not be the framer's fault as we shall see in greater detail.

The same effect as a rounded cut from miter saw wobble is also produced in sanding the ends before gluing, a must whenever a hand-operated saw and miter box are used. Even with the moulding length firmly braced and the sandpaper mounted on a flat block, sanding by hand will give an uneven pressure which will round at least the very edges of the cut. A power-driven sander with miter guide will give an exact sanding job, but almost anyone who has a power sander usually has the bench saw which, with the proper blade, makes sanding unnecessary. To repeat; always sand the cut from hand-operated saws cautiously.

It might be well to mention another problem here, one which arises from the type of material being cut rather than from any errors in cutting or in sanding the mitered ends of the moulding. The type of moulding called **linen liner** (or any fabric-covered moulding) presents a peculiar problem to the framer. When cut by a handsaw, cloth will fray at the cut edge. The coarser the saw teeth, the worse the fraying. When the joint is made, this fraying presents a very unwelcome appearance and can ruin an otherwise excellent job.

The chopper mentioned previously has been favored by some framers for precisely this one advantage, that it will slice fabrics very cleanly so that the joint is almost invisible. However, experience has shown that the high-speed bench saw with a smooth-cut, hollow-ground blade will cut fabric-covered mouldings just as cleanly as the chopper and give results fully as acceptable. The elimination of this problem for the framer with a handsaw is impossible, but it can be reduced to the minimum by the following method: With the moulding in the miter box and held so that it will not shift position, place the saw gently down on the moulding. Using a pencil with a fine point, make a faint line across the fabric—just let the pencil follow the saw teeth. Remove the saw, and with a mat knife or some equally sharp blade, cut carefully through the fabric along the indicated line. Then make the cut in the usual way. The cutting by the knife will have severed the fabric threads and prevent raveling or fraying on the part of the moulding which will be used in the frame. The other side, of course, will fray, but since this is the reverse angle, it cannot be used in making a frame and so the fraying will not matter.

In measuring the frame for cutting, keep in mind that it is the size of the rabbeted part which counts. The illustration below shows a cross section of a typical piece of moulding. Note especially the rabbet and the lip, for these parts must always be to the inside. It is not uncommon for the beginner to turn the moulding the wrong way, making a reverse cut and thereby spoiling a length of moulding. In expensive types, such carelessness is costly.

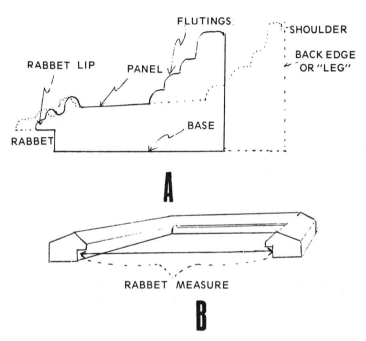

RABBET MEASURE

B

It is the rabbet or indentation in the back of the moulding which holds the glass and other components of the assembled work or, in the case of oil paintings, the stretcher bar and canvas. The cutting must therefore be the **inner** measurement from **rabbet edge to rabbet edge.** The outer, visible window area does not count nor do the outside dimensions, as these depend on width of rabbeting and width of moulding, respectively. The dotted lines in the diagram above show how these might vary.

Diagram B shows how the measurement should be made to determine the size of the frame. Let us say, for example, that a watercolor is to be matted and then framed under glass.

The size of the watercolor is 16 by 20 inches, and we want 3 inches of matting showing around it on all sides. The mat must overlap the watercolor about ⅛ inch in order to fasten the one against the other. Say that the width of the rabbet in the moulding we have chosen is ¼ inch and the width of the moulding itself is 3 inches. This latter width is not important in the cutting as it does not affect the measurement at all.

In order to have 3 inches of mat showing through the glass, we must have an additional ¼ inch to fit into the rabbet (see below) on each side. Then there are 3 inches of mat on each side, and the work is 20 inches wide **minus** the ⅛ inch overlap on each side. Thus one length will be 20 plus 3 plus 3 plus ¼ plus ¼ **minus** ⅛ **minus** ⅛ for 26¼ inches total from inside rabbet edge to inside rabbet edge, as shown below. This then

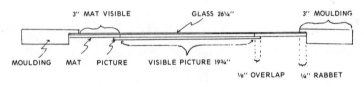

(CROSS SECTION NOT TO SCALE)

will be the measurement desired for cutting. The other length will be 16 plus 3 plus 3 plus ¼ plus ¼ **minus** ⅛ **minus** ⅛ for 22¼ inches total. The measurement inside the back of the lip (the rabbet measurement) will thus be 22¼ x 26¼ inches.

If just the moulding were to be used to frame an oil painting, for example, and there were no liner to consider, the lip would overlap the canvas edge ¼ inch. The inner measurement (rabbet) would then be the size of the canvas, 16 x 20 inches, and the lip would cover or overlap ¼ inch of the canvas on all sides. It would be like this:

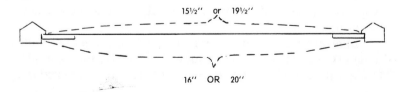

If a type of liner is to be used, the liner would be 16 x 20 inches and the outer or "capping" moulding would have to make allowance on each side for this additional width as shown below. We assume that the linen liner is 2 inches wide total. For this type of framing, measure the **outside** lengths of the finished liner before cutting for the outer capping. In this case, both the liner and the outer capping would be cut on the saw and joined as individual components of the finished frame. Check the liner to make sure it fits the painting before

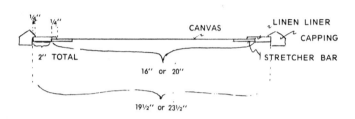

the capping is cut. Techniques for using the linen liner with capping will be explained in the section on assembling.

One other point should be mentioned with regard to multiple frames, either those with linen liners for oils or compound frames made up of two or more tiers of moulding. Make the first one up as a regular frame to fit the work. When that is joined, measure it for the next tier or capping **as if it were the work to be framed,** i.e., take the **outside** measurements. If more mouldings are to be added, treat each step the same way. It is better to do this step by step because there are always inaccuracies and variations in even the most skilled and careful workmanship. Unless the work is done step by step there is too much chance that the final capping will be too small or too large to fit the moulding of the previous step.

The illustrations show where the measurement must be made on the moulding strip for proper cutting. Both A and B

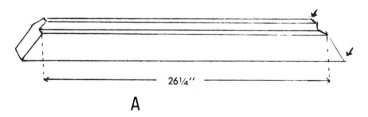

A

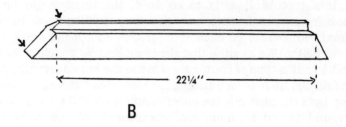

B

show the final measurement would be 22¼ x 26¼ inches. Measurements made from either the lip edge or the back edge of the moulding as indicated by the dotted lines will **not** give the correct lengths when the frame is joined.

How long a piece of moulding would be needed to cut these lengths? And don't forget that you will need **two** of each since the frame has four sides. The length needed to cut **one** side is the length of that side **plus double** the width of the moulding. Double because there are two miter cuts, one for each end. The diagram below shows a length of moulding with dotted lines to show how much is lost. Roughly, the loss at each cut is equal to the width of the moulding. More precisely, it is the

THE BRACKETED LENGTHS ARE EQUAL

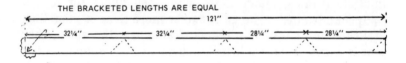

width of the moulding **minus** the width of the rabbet, but since the saw blade takes about ⅛ inch for its kerf (width of cut) it is necessary to allow for that also. The amount of waste caused by allowing full width of the moulding for the miter cut is negligible. For our sample 16 x 20 watercolor requiring lengths of 22¼ x 26¼ inches, using the 3-inch wide moulding, we would need two lengths of 28¼ each and two lengths of 32¼ inches each. We have found it a good idea to allow a bit more if possible so that a chip or splinter on the right-hand cut can be eliminated by recutting and still have enough left for cutting the right length.

The total length of moulding required to make such a frame is therefore **twice** 28¼ inches plus **twice** 32¼ inches for a total of 121 inches--10 feet 1 inch in all. A safer amount to figure on would be 10 ft. 4 or 10 ft. 6 inches. This is particularly true if you are using a **compo** moulding which is liable to chip in cutting.

It might be advisable to discuss compo mouldings somewhat at this point, as they are common among finished mouldings. These mouldings are of wood coated with a composition material such as gesso (a gypsum or plaster of Paris compound) which can be moulded into patterns and designs while fresh and then allowed to harden. After this coating has hardened, it is finished either with a gloss paint, a gold or other leafing, or in any other type finish which is desired. The reason for using the composition layer is that it can be run through dies or moulding mills to mass produce filigrees and ornate designs which would be prohibitively expensive and not so uniform if done by hand. The mouldings are generally beautiful in pattern, but they present a difficulty for the framer in that they tend to flake or chip when cut because the composition (**compo**) layer is very brittle. They are not recommended for the beginner, but with practice, and by utilizing the following suggestions, the average framer will have little difficulty with them.

An initial bit of advice is that these compos cannot successfully be handled by hand-cutting methods. A 10-inch bench saw is the minimum which should be used although the 8- or 9-inch can be used if the moulding is not too high. If a heavy compo moulding is being cut, say 3 or 4 inches wide with a shoulder of perhaps 2½ inches, even the 10-inch blade will not be able to cut it properly by the time the moulding is on a miter guide jig, because the effective cutting height of the blade will be only about 2½ inches, less if blade stabilizers are being used, and this will usually cause large chunks of compo to chip off the top of the moulding. With this as with any other moulding, the saw blade should come well above the top of the moulding being cut. This is not only a necessity for clean cutting of the moulding, but is a necessary safety precaution lest the moulding should bind over the saw blade, break, and cause a serious accident.

The blade used for cutting compo mouldings should be very sharp and be of the smooth-cut or fine-cut hollow-ground variety. The carbides are successful only if they have about 48 teeth or more on a 10-inch blade.

Once this is set up for cutting, the next step is to tape the moulding. Masking tape is best. Put the length of moulding in place on the left-hand miter guide as shown below so that the angle of cut is established. Then run a ½ or ¾ inch masking tape strip from **under** the lip of the rabbet up and across the moulding and down the back to the base. Be sure the tape goes all the way down the back, as compo mouldings are coated even on the back and chipping here will be visible. Press the tape down firmly into all the ornamentation and design. The dotted lines show how the tape should go across the compo moulding in line with the saw blade and where the cut is to be made. The cut will be made **directly through** the tape. After the cut, the remaining piece of tape should be carefully removed; **carefully** because it can peel off gold leaf if not removed gently. Also, should there be a large chip which comes off with the tape, and this **does** happen, the chip can be gently removed and reglued into place on the moulding.

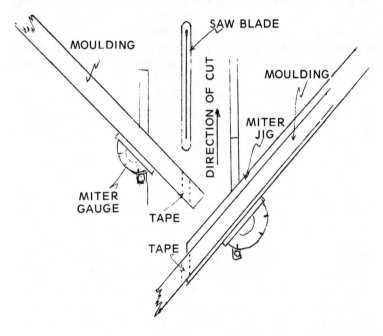

It will be noted that by running the tape at this 45 deg angle it is no longer in line with the saw cut when it reaches the back of the moulding. This is compensated for by holding the tape in place at the top of the shoulder and then straightening the piece to go vertically down the back. This will leave a wrinkle of excess tape at the top, which does not matter. It is well to practice on a piece of scrap if such is available before attempting to work on good moulding.

Once the cutting has been accomplished, moulding sections have to be joined. As previously explained, this can be done in any of several ways. They can be joined one corner at a time using a miter vise or a woodworker's vise (or metalworking vise if the jaws are covered so they won't damage the moulding). If compo or delicately finished mouldings are to be joined, it is always best to face the clamp jaws either with cardboard or soft plastic to protect the moulding finish. The method of joining here is to put glue on both miter cuts, put them together in the vise and tighten it to hold them in place. Then nail and countersink the nails. After this, the corner can be removed and another corner joined. But we do **not** recommend joining one corner at a time, even though many professional framers do. First, if the vise is of the jaw type and you have not applied sufficient pressure, the moulding may be driven out of the jaws when the nailing begins. Even if not pounded out of the jaws, the moulding might be damaged by some amount of slippage. Second, if a compo moulding is being used, there is too much risk of excess clamp pressure cracking the compo coat and ruining the moudling.

There is further objection to this single joint system in that it does not give any way of checking the square of the finished product without applying the try square nor can it be used to correct **minor** curvature or warp in the moulding. And, since only the nails are holding the joint until the glue has set, any tendency for the corner to separate while the glue is wet cannot be stopped. This is aggravated by the fact that the frame must be handled for each corner joint.

We have found the use of four corner clamps invaluable and recommend it for anyone, especially the beginner. In this system first one corner is glued and joined but not nailed and then the **diagonal** corner, indicated on the next page. When these two corners are joined, all four clampst are set up and the frame clamped as it will be for the final joining. If no warpage shows up, which cannot be corrected in the clamps, both remaining joints receive glue and are reclamped into place. The four corners are then nailed and countersunk, and the entire frame, still in four clamps, is left until the glue sets. It is better to leave the frame overnight, especially if it's a large, heavy one.

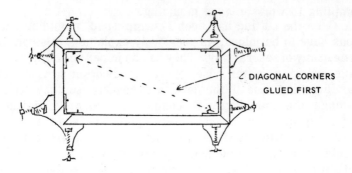

∠ DIAGONAL CORNERS
GLUED FIRST

This four-clamp system has proven very successful because one can check against warp, twist, or curvature before the final nailing is done. If any side proves defective, or any miter cut is inaccurate, it can be redone without tearing apart a joined and nailed frame. The use of all four clamps is also a fine check on the square of the frame.

After the frame is removed from the clamps and checked to make certain that it is as it should be in all respects, the touching up should be done. First the corners should be sanded with fine sandpaper if there is any roughness and then the finish retouched. Gold-leafed or gold-painted mouldings should have a gilding rubbed over them to cover the compo or wood underneath and to fill up the minute cracks of the mitered joints. If a bronze powder or any material which will tarnish in time is used, a coat of lacquer or plastic spray should be given as protection against oxidation.

The nail holes and any small cracks or flaws should be filled with the appropriate filler of as near the correct color as possible. As was mentioned before, the sticks sold for touching up finished panels work very well for this purpose.

There are a number of mouldings and finishes which require additional treatment before joining, as they are very difficult to retouch afterward. Chief among these are the black mouldings, whether with or without a compo base. Black mouldings tend to show a light streak at the joint which, after gluing and nailing, is most difficult to correct or hide. Use of the black marking crayons or black retouch compounds is always noticeable. For this reason, it is best to mark the portion of the moulding indicated in the shaded area on the diagram below with black marking ink **before** joining. In every case, it is the edge which must be colored. This gives a joint in which no noticeable line is present. The same may be done with dark woods, using a brown marking pencil, and the gilding wax may be used for joints on gold-finish moulding. But you must remember to use the least amount of such color fillers on the surface of the cuts or it will have a weakening

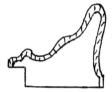

effect on the corner joint by reducing the adhesive area available for the glue. This is one of the reasons why we strongly recommend the use of nails as added strength despite many claims for adhesives that with their use nails are not necessary for joining. The size and type of moulding plus the size of the frame will be determining factors in how the joints or corners should be nailed, but usually two nails per joint will suffice. Most mouldings are thicker toward the back or shoulder and smaller toward the lip or front. If the size brad which serves for the nailing at the back is too heavy to use toward the lip without danger of splitting the wood, use a smaller brad. Always drill first, before nailing. The advantages of two nails rather than one is that they provide more strength, and can, if there has been a slight curve or twist in the moulding, help to correct this. The following figures show several mouldings in cross section and how nailing would be

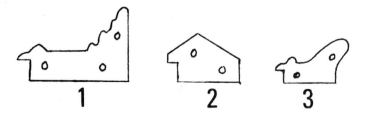

1   2   3

31

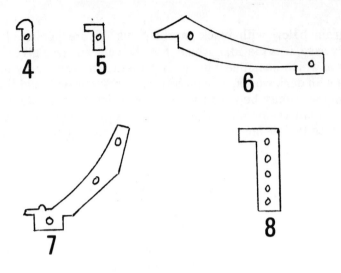

done when they are joined. Obviously the larger mouldings will use heavier brads or nails and will generally provide ample space for three nails. The small mouldings will be used for small framing jobs and, since there is little room for nailing, are usually best joined with only one nail as shown in sketches 4 and 5 above. An exception to this is the deep, narrow capping, as in sketch 8 above, where the thickness of the moulding does not permit large nails but where the moulding type will be used on larger works. These joints are nailed by using a row of four or five smaller nails which, totally, give an equivalent support strength.

At one time **cross nailing** was the accepted practice but this has given way in general to the system of nailing from one direction only. Especially in fragile mouldings, there is a risk of splitting the moulding lengths because of the nails penetrating from two directions and because one nail often hits another and is driven off at an angle. The next diagram shows examples of unidirectional nailing (A), cross-nailing (B), and the result when one nail hits into another from the right angle (C).

In some cases, however, especially if the frame is very heavy or if there is a tendency to gap at the joint because of moulding warp or curvature, cross nailing is desirable and should be done. Also, if there is any possibility that the weight of glass or other components in a frame may exert undue stress on the alternate corners, cross nailing of at least the two

32

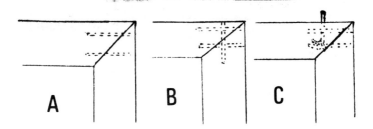

A B C

diagonally opposed corners in question is desirable, as shown below, to provide support against the downward pull of the weight on the joint. Take care that the **cross nail** is not in line with the other two nails or the moulding may be split, as in diagram C above.

Sketch 8 in the previous diagram on nailing (repeated below) shows a type of moulding known as **capping** which is very popular for framing modern works. It has a deep leg, usually around 1¼ inch, with a narrow facing of approximately ½ inch. This is often used for works of a size

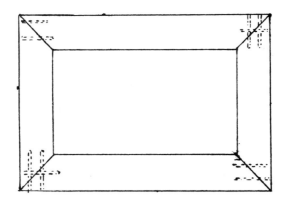

which, especially if glassed, have a weight greater than the moulding will safely support. The use of four or five nails will be adequate only up to a point. Beyond that, more secure bracing of the corners is necessary. One type, the narrow angle bracing on the back of the legs, as shown next, can be done at any time but preferably as soon as the corners are set and the clamps removed.

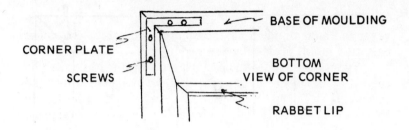

CORNER PLATE

SCREWS

BASE OF MOULDING

BOTTOM
VIEW OF CORNER

RABBET LIP

This type of support is limited by the thickness of the moulding, obviously, and has the added disadvantage of only bracing the **back** edge of the moulding. Frames braced in this manner can open at the front after a time and, although they will hold together, they are unsightly. Another system is that shown below where the angle brace is not the flat L-plate but the corner brace. This allows a wider, heavier type brace to be used, and in a position where the frame corner will have support at its center. Needless to emphasize, they are sturdy enough for any purpose, being limited only by the size of the screw which can be used. This is a very good type of support for cappings on works under glass. Its only disadvantage is

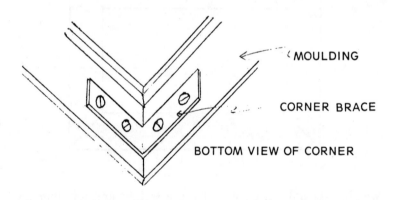

MOULDING

CORNER BRACE

BOTTOM VIEW OF CORNER

that it must be put on **after** the work has been assembled and mounted in the frame because the work cannot be put in after the braces are in place. Equally, if for any reason the work is to be removed, the braces must be removed first.

This type of corner brace is not needed for framing canvases as the frame can be attached directly to the stretcher bar, which will provide adequate support.

From time to time, you may run into problems created by curved mouldings or by the fact that the unaided frame (and this is especially true of the capping style) just isn't physically strong enough to do the job expected of it. When this happens, it is necessary to brace or crossbrace the frame from the back. This is something which obviously must be done after the work to be framed has been assembled in the frame. The figure A below shows the simplest type of bracing. This is a wooden strip running from top to bottom to provide additional support.

BACK VIEW OF FRAME

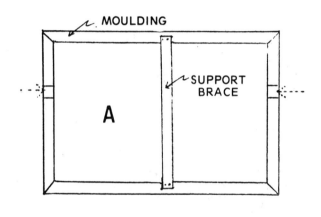

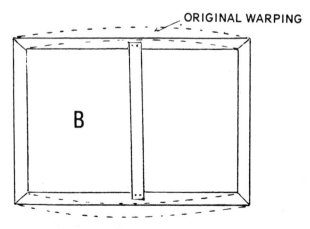

This same type could be used if, as in B, the problem had been curvature in the moulding which must be pulled together at the center to make the frame sides parallel. The original position is indicated by the dashed lines.

This type of brace running from top to bottom will prevent the frame from hanging flat against the wall and will produce a side to side wobble. This can be eliminated by the use of two blocks in the back, as indicated by the dotted arrows in figure A, or by use of two braces, one toward either end, instead of just one in the center, but this procedure still holds the frame away from the wall. It is better if the strip(s) can be inset in the moulding, as shown below.

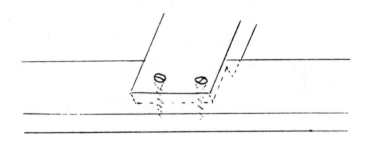

Where that is not practical, as in the case of narrow moulding such as capping, the use of a strip (brace) of wood just long enough to go from side to side and fastened **inside** the frame is excellent. The fastening is done as shown in sketch A

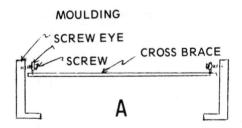

MOULDING
SCREW EYE
SCREW
CROSS BRACE

A

above by using a screw eye (or two) at either end of the brace and running a screw through this eye and into the moulding

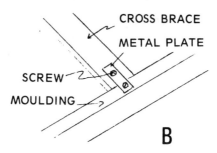

CROSS BRACE
METAL PLATE
SCREW
MOULDING

B

strip. Again, two such braces may be used if necessary. For flatter moulding, strips of metal can be fastened from the brace to the back of the moulding, as shown in B above.

For larger works, it may sometimes be advisable to crossbrace them in the manner of the larger stretcher bars used by painters. This is shown below. If the crossed bar or

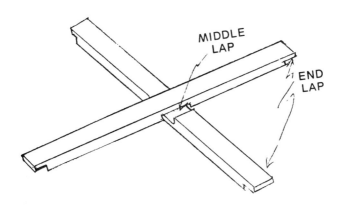

MIDDLE LAP

END LAP

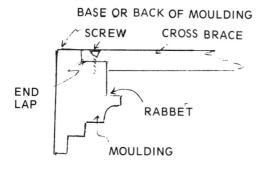

BASE OR BACK OF MOULDING

SCREW   CROSS BRACE

END LAP

RABBET

MOULDING

strips can be set down into the frame as with cappings, one can rest atop the other with no difficulty. If the space is too shallow, as in most mouldings, the crosspieces must be middle-lapped so that they can fit together and so that both are on the same plane. This can be done with a saw and wood chisel. The lapped ends can then either be nailed or screwed to the sides of the frame or, for a better job, inset into the moulding as described previously.

The best structural brace for large and heavy mouldings is the flat L-brace at each corner as shown in the diagram below. These prevent the dust cover from going on neatly, if

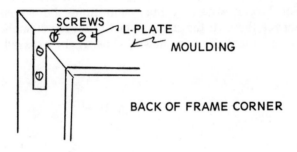

the dust cover is to be used, unless the paper is cut out around them, or these L-braces can be inset to make them flush with the back of the moulding and thus invisible. To do this, lay the braces in the position desired, mark around them with a pencil and then chisel out inside the marked area to the proper depth to accommodate the L-brace. Then the corner plate is set in place, marked for screws and removed so that the screw holes may be bored. After that, the plate is returned to its position and the screws put in. Naturally, it is far simpler to just put the brace on at the very last, after the dust cover, eliminating the work of insetting.

The techniques required to make composite frames of liners and mouldings or of several different types of moulding follow the same general procedures. For example, to fasten a liner into a walnut capping, make the capping to fit around the liner and use screw eyes and screws (as shown next just as we discussed for fastening braces into capping. It will be ap-

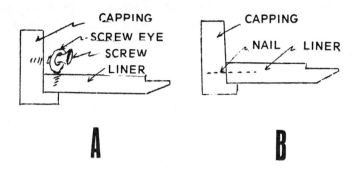

parent that nailing could be, and often is, used. Since handling
the framed work by the capping will, however, pull the nails
into or through the moulding, as indicated by the dotted lines
in B above, this is not a satisfactory way of handling the
problem.

If the liner is thicker than the rabbeting in the moulding,
the arrangement shown below must be used. Again, nailing

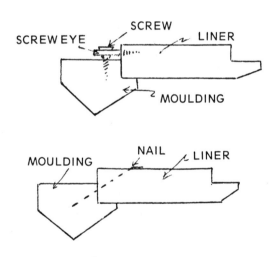

could be used but it is not secure. In the method, above screw
eyes are put into the liner or stretcher bar (if the work is an
original oil) and then screwed to the moulding. The use of nails
to fasten a liner or, especially, an original oil on a stretcher
bar into a frame, is perfectly adequate when the moulding is
wide and strong enough so that it will not bend or give with
handling.

In some cases, where the original oil will protrude beyond the back of the moulding, a thin lathing strip can be stained or painted and put all around to conceal the edges of the stretcher where the canvas folds over. This is shown in the diagrams below. This stripping need not be miter-cut and can be simply fixed on with brads. It must be cut and fastened onto the stretcher before any measurements are made for the final framing. The technique of stripping should be used with **floating** frames, a type to be discussed later.

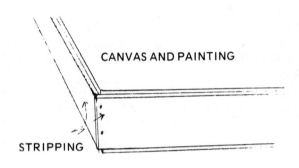

CANVAS AND PAINTING

STRIPPING

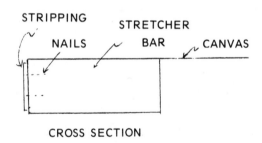

STRIPPING   STRETCHER

NAILS   BAR   CANVAS

CROSS SECTION

Before any further discussion of the types of mouldings and how to handle them in cutting miters, it will be necessary to turn our attention to the project of making a miter jig for accurate measurement of moulding lengths when making the second miter cut. For those using the handsaw and miter box, this will have no importance. For those using the bench saw, it will be one of the most imporatnt considerations in framing.

Constructing a Miter Jig for Framing

The miter jig is not a complicated piece of equipment and can be built quite simply and quickly from basic materials. It will save you untold hours of time and will guarantee the best results. Despite its simplicity, it is a tool which must be of the utmost accuracy, as every length of moulding cut for a frame will be affected by this jig. Its purpose, of course, is to measure the proper length of moulding in place for accurate cutting of the miter. It will be useful first to examine the basic process of cutting before going on to the actual building of the jig.

Moulding lengths can either be cut from precut pieces which are not mitered but are just a bit larger than the length needed after allowance is made for the two miter cuts as we saw in Chapter 2, or they can be cut from longer lengths without precutting. The advantage in the latter approach is that it reduces the number of cuts which must be made and, if any mistake is made or a flaw in the moulding discovered, only so much length will be wasted as is needed to correct this. With a precut piece, the whole length might well be useless. The disadvantage of cutting from a long length is primarily that it is more difficult to handle. In either case, though, the cutting will be done in the same manner.

First, the right-hand cut is made on the left miter gauge of the saw as shown on the following page. This mitered end is then placed firmly against the stop block on the miter guide jig so that the accurate and proper length will be measured out, and the left-hand miter cut is made. Since the bed of the miter jig is higher than the level of the saw table, it is convenient to place a runner strip of equal height along the table, parallel to the saw blade, for the length of moulding to slide along. Without this runner strip, there is risk of accident (and damaged moulding) from the moulding bending against the saw blade as the cut progresses and binding it. If the moulding

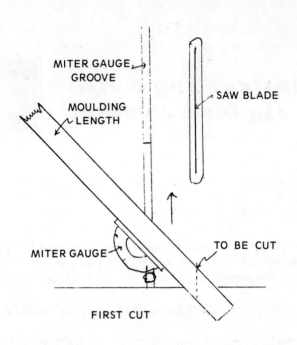

MITER GAUGE GROOVE

SAW BLADE

MOULDING LENGTH

MITER GAUGE

TO BE CUT

FIRST CUT

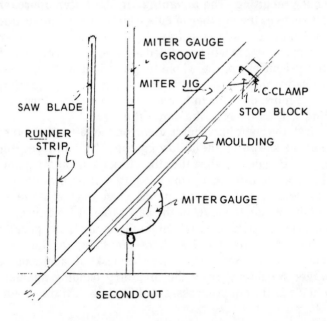

MITER GAUGE GROOVE

MITER JIG

C-CLAMP

STOP BLOCK

SAW BLADE

RUNNER STRIP

MOULDING

MITER GAUGE

SECOND CUT

is very long or heavy, it is wise to also support the leftover section with your hand. This manipulation of the long moulding stick is the chief reason why you might prefer precut lengths. If the moulding is a large compo or wide hardwood, precutting is always recommended.

To build the jig in its simplest form, you will need:

1 Miter guide or gauge
1 Wood strip 5 or 6 feet long, 4½ inches wide, ¾ inch thick
1 Wood strip same length as above, 2½ inches wide, ¾ inch thick
2 Bolts ⅝ inch long, with washers and nuts
5 or 6 Wood screws 1½ or 2 inches long
And appropriate tools.

The above are variable measurements and those given are recommended but not insisted upon. The base strip will work satisfactorily if it is 4 inches wide and only 5 feet long, and the back strip will be adequate for most work if only 2 inches high. They must both be the same length, however, and ¾ inch thick. Thinner boards will not have sufficient rigidity for general work. All instructions given below for making the jig will assume the measurements of materials as given above and must be modified when necessary if different materials are used. The wood lengths **MUST BE WELL SEASONED AND ABSOLUTELY STRAIGHT**. Any curvature at all in either piece will make it useless for this jig.

Diagram I is an extended drawing of how the pieces will be fitted together. Backing strip A will be bolted to the face of

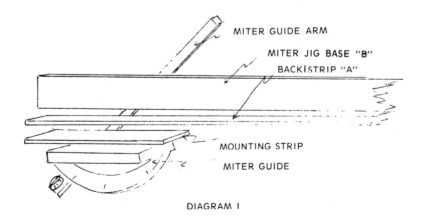

MITER GUIDE ARM
MITER JIG BASE "B"
BACK STRIP "A"
MOUNTING STRIP
MITER GUIDE

DIAGRAM I

the miter guide. Base strip B is fastened to A by means of the wood screws placed 1 foot apart along the total length of the strips.

Diagram II represents a cross section of the assembled jig showing respective placement of miter guide, back strip A, and base strip B. Note that base strip B rests on the arm of the miter guide.

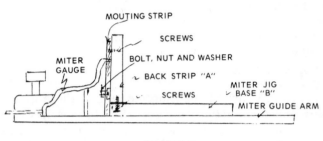

DIAGRAM II

Strips A and B are fitted very carefully together and aligned. It is best at this point if they can be clamped together either by use of a vise or C-clamps. An alternate system is to nail strip A to strip B at one end and then, after carefully aligning them at the other end, nail that also. When the two are held firmly together, bore holes 1 foot apart but NOT close to the end which will be the miter end. It is well to put the first screw about 6 inches back from this end. See Diagram III. The holes must be countersunk so that none of the screw heads will protrude below the level of the wood as this would cause them to scratch into the saw bench and would prevent the jig from being absolutely flat to the surface. The screws should then be put in. Next the assembled wooden element is placed against the face plate on the miter guide as shown in Diagram II. Marks are made through the holes in the miter guide face to indicate where the bolts will go through the wood, back strip A, to hold it into place against the miter guide. Referring to Diagram IV, note that the miter end of the wood element **must** extend sufficiently beyond the edge of the miter guide to allow for the cutting off of the end of the jig when it has been fastened to the miter guide. The end indicated by the dotted

44

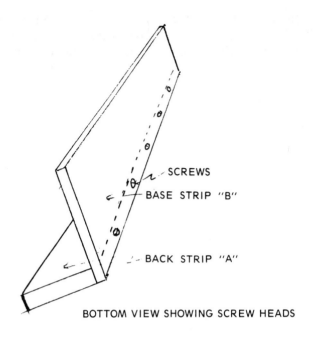

SCREWS

BASE STRIP "B"

BACK STRIP "A"

BOTTOM VIEW SHOWING SCREW HEADS

DIAGRAM III

lines will be cut off as soon as the wooden element is firmly fixed to the guide.

Bore holes through back strip A at the places indicated and then countersink from the **front** of strip A for the washer and nut. If the miter guide does not have holes through the

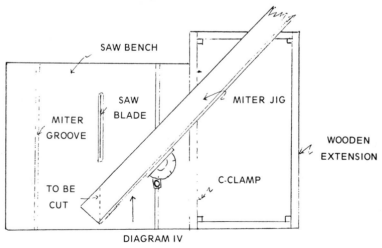

SAW BENCH

SAW BLADE

MITER JIG

MITER GROOVE

WOODEN EXTENSION

TO BE CUT

C-CLAMP

DIAGRAM IV

facing, these must be bored in and then the measurement made for boring through strip A. When this is accomplished, put the bolts through the holes in the miter guide facing and then through the holes in back strip A. See Diagram V. Place the washer over the bolt, put on the nuts, and tighten them into place.

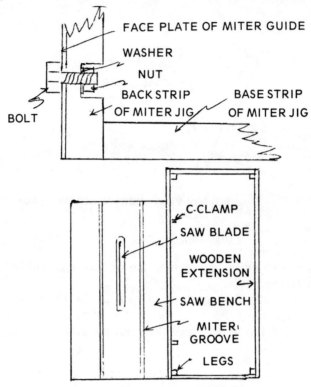

FACE PLATE OF MITER GUIDE

WASHER

NUT

BACK STRIP
OF MITER JIG

BASE STRIP
OF MITER JIG

BOLT

C-CLAMP

SAW BLADE

WOODEN
EXTENSION

SAW BENCH

MITER
GROOVE

LEGS

TOP VIEW—EXTENSION RIGHT HAND CUTTING

DIAGRAM V

Now set the miter guide to a 45 deg angle as shown in Diagram IV. This discussion is for right-handed operation. In this case, the final cut on the moulding length is most conveniently made on the right-hand side of the saw. For LEFT-HANDED use, it might be more convenient to make the final cut on the left-hand side of the saw. In that case, the left miter guide and the right-hand miter jig will be interchanged. The miter jig would have to be constructed for left-hand operation. See Diagram VI.

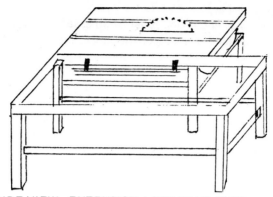

SIDE VIEW—EXTENSION LEFT HAND CUTTING

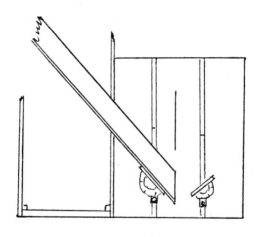

TOP VIEW—LEFT HAND CUTTING

DIAGRAM VI

With the miter guide at 45 deg and firmly fixed in position (and check this carefully against a protractor, try square with 45 deg set on it, or any other accurate device) push the jig through the saw blade. See Diagram IV. This will cut off the end of the jig at EXACTLY the point where future sticks of moulding will be cut off by the same blade, and this will be the beginning mark for the measurements along the jig for future use.

Two points of caution must be stressed. First, if any other saw blade is used in place of the initial one, a check must be made to see that it hits the miter end of the jig exactly. A carbide blade, for example, has a wider kerf or cut than the hollow-ground blade. Changing to a carbide blade, therefore, would throw all measurements off and make the moulding approximately 1/16 inch shorter than with the hollow-ground blade. Conversely, use of the hollow-ground after the carbide if the carbide were used to make the miter cut on the jig, would make the moulding length about 1/16 inch **longer**, as the hollow-ground blade takes less cutting width. The first example would also, naturally, cut away a bit of the miter jig. Needless to say, perhaps, both situations can be compensated for, but only with difficulty. The blade of the saw cannot be moved parallel without use of washers on the shaft, something **not** recommended for the amateur, nor can the miter jig be shifted at all without dismantling it and reboring the holes or by making them oval in the beginning. This is also to be avoided. It is obviously best to make the jig with the type of blade which will be used throughout for cutting the moulding and then to keep this as the standard blade when using the jig.

The second point of caution is that the 45 deg angle of the miter jig must be absolutely accurate when the cut is made. It can be corrected later, but this often leads to cutting off more of the jig end with subsequent necessity to revise the measurement markings along the jig. If you want to weld the miter guide at 45 deg to insure its permanent placement you may, but this is not necessary and limits any future use of the miter guide except for cutting 45 deg angles. It is sufficient to check the guide angle from time to time to make certain that handling has not changed the angle to more or less than 45 deg.

When the end of the miter jig has been cut off, it is time to begin the marking of the jig base for quick measurement of moulding lengths. This is best done by very carefully measuring along the outer edge of base strip B as shown next. It is sufficient to mark each ¼ inch unless your tools are very accurate. In that case, you might mark every ⅛ inch. For most nonprofessional work, the ¼ inch is perfectly adequate and makes working easier. The ⅛ inch "marks," when needed, can be judged by eye accurately enough.

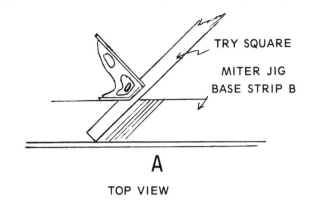

TRY SQUARE

MITER JIG

BASE STRIP B

A

TOP VIEW

NUMBERED INCHES

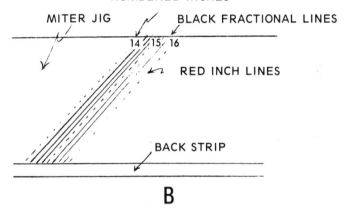

MITER JIG   BLACK FRACTIONAL LINES

14 15 16

RED INCH LINES

BACK STRIP

B

After the edge is marked, take the try square, and, using the 45 deg arrangement, draw lines from the edge marks back to the back strip as indicated in the diagram above. Mark these with the appropriate readings as indicated, making the inch marks in red if desired. Red inch markings help to make reading easier. The black lines as well as the red lines can be made with ballpoint pens, pressing them down so that the line is also pressed into the wood. When this has been done, the jig is finished and ready for use.

For someone planning to do quite a lot of framing and wanting a permanent jig, it is not necessary to use the expensive adjustable miter guide as included in the above. A bar of the same size as the arm of the miter guide so that it will ride firmly in the groove on the saw bench, can be affixed with a strip of sheet or angle iron welded on at 45 deg, as shown below. This can be bored to take bolts the same as the face of the miter guide and is perfectly satisfactory. It should not be

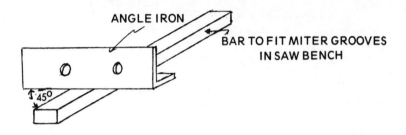

necessary to check such an arrangement for angle accuracy as with the adjustable miter guide.

Whether the 5 foot or the 6 foot lengths of wood were used for making the miter jig, the longest length of it will extend over the edge of the average saw bench. If a supporting table has been built around the bench saw to support longer pieces, there will be no problem. If, however, the saw bench is just of standard size, some kind of extension must be fixed to either side so that the moulding lengths and the miter jig can be handled easily. Some extension grids are available for saw benches, but most of them are not really wide enough for the framer's purpose. Either a table must be built on both sides of the saw bench or a support added, wide enough to support long moulding strips and the miter jig. The support, no matter which kind, must be level and must be the exact same height as the saw bench. The following figure indicates one possibility in making such a support.

The two support legs rest on the floor, the inner side of the rectangle is clamped to the saw bench with C-clamps for easy removal. One of these on either side is sufficient if there is no table.

Only one other thing remains to be done. A stop block must be made to clamp onto the miter jig so that the moulding can be held in its exact position without wavering or creeping while being cut and so that two or more pieces of exactly the same length can be cut. This is a simple block cut with reverse

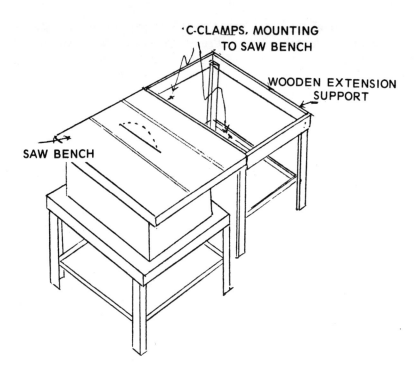

·C-CLAMPS, MOUNTING
TO SAW BENCH

WOODEN EXTENSION
SUPPORT

SAW BENCH

miter as shown in the diagram below, and it's held in place
with a small C-clamp. This stop block can be adjusted for any
length merely by loosening the clamp and sliding the block
along the back strip.

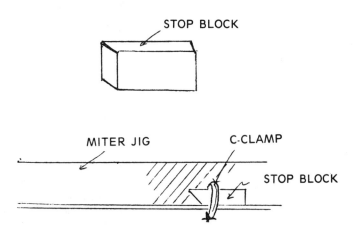

STOP BLOCK

MITER JIG   C-CLAMP

STOP BLOCK

A word about how to measure the proper moulding length. You must remember that you're not interested in the length of the moulding along the inner lip nor along the outer shoulder **but along the edge of the rabbeting,** as we said before. A look at the diagram below will show the proper position of the end of the moulding for a 1/16-inch moulding strip, and the position of the stop block. You will see from this that with narrow

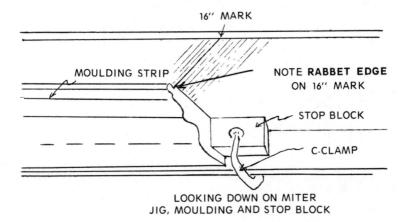

LOOKING DOWN ON MITER
JIG, MOULDING AND STOP BLOCK

moulding the stop block will be closer to the rabbet than with wider mouldings and that there will be variations with various depths of rabbeting. The stop block position for a 1 16-inch length of ½-inch wide moulding will thus be different from its position when cutting a 1/16-inch length from 3-inch wide moulding. The system, once understood and used, is very simple and will give no trouble at all.

One special type of moulding merits a special note, and that is the so-called 'shadow-box' moulding. This moulding, shown below, has a **double** rabbet so that the work can be

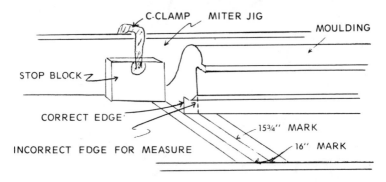

mounted a significant distance behind the glass. A work which measures 16 x 20 would fit the **rear or lower** rabbet and the glass would be smaller—to fit the upper or front rabbet. To cut this, you must measure the lower or back rabbet in order to get the proper dimensions. The smaller opening in the front due to the second rabbet would of course reduce the amount of the work seen. As we will note in the chapter on matting, to show a certain dimension from the front requires taking into account the difference in width of the front rabbet.

The following diagram shows where the moulding would be placed on the miter jig to obtain a 16-inch length for the back rabbet. The upper or front rabbet would make the glass size correspondingly smaller.

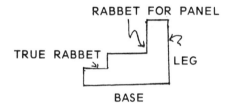

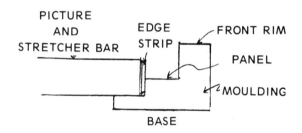

Another type of double rabbeted moulding is that used in creating the floating frame. This, as shown next, makes use of the two rabbets but in a different manner than the shadow box. In the floating frame, the rabbeting faces outward and the distance between the rabbet edges acts as a separator to create an illusion of discontinuity between the painting edge and the outer edge of the frame. It is essential to place this correctly when cutting and to remember that it is of a shape which might easily deceive you into placing it incorrectly for cutting. The diagram below shows the proper place for making measurements in using this moulding. Note especially that the canvas goes into the moulding from the **front** rather

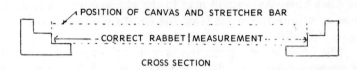

POSITION OF CANVAS AND STRETCHER BAR

CORRECT RABBET | MEASUREMENT

CROSS SECTION

than from the back and that this type of moulding cannot be used for things framed under glass unless it is used only as a capping around an inner element.

Once again, you are reminded that the raw edges of the canvas should be concealed by thin wood stripping before measurements are made for the floating frame.

Handling Basic Moulding Styles

If all the mouldings made were flat or square with only right angles, you would have few problems other than poor-quality moulding and its defects. However, a great many of the more attractive mouldings have no right angles at all (except in the rabbeting if the rabbet is properly cut) and hence require development of techniques not usually required for cutting construction mouldings or in cabinet work.

Our first general category of mouldings, which for convenience, we designate as Type A, are those which have a simple right angle formed by the back and the base as shown by the dotted lines in the examples below. If these are properly rabbeted, they will have parallel surfaces of back and rabbet

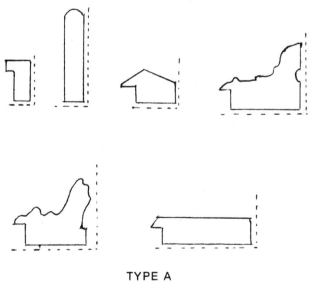

TYPE A

face and will be simple to join in the clamps. As we shall see later, not all moulding is carefully cut and the rabbeting angle is not 90 deg. This will not impair proper cutting, but it will make joining very difficult and at times impossible, discussed later. All the above Type A mouldings should be simple to cut and simple to join.

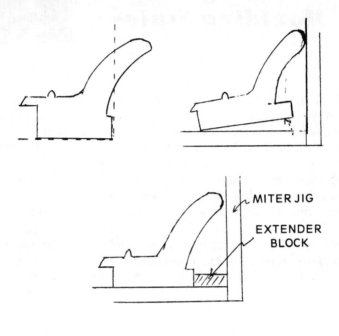

TYPE B

The Type B moulding is also quite simple to join by use of an additional block as indicated in the diagram above. The significant feature of this moulding from the framer's point of view is that the upper edge of the shoulder extends out further than the lower, squared part of the moulding base. If this moulding is held flat with the back edge of the shoulder pressed firmly against the back strip A of the miter jig—or against the face of the miter guide—the cut could also be made simple. However, in many cases, the rounded contour of the shoulder allows this moulding to "lift" upward as pressure is applied from the front and the moulding raises in back from the flat position. This angular change is shown in exaggerated form in the diagram. Use of the extender block, as shown, effectively lengthens the base of the moulding so that the back of the shoulder does not touch the back rest of the miter jig or guide and so cannot "lift" the moulding. This extender block can be of any practical width just so it is wide enough to provide clearance for the back of the shoulder, and it should be at least one-third the length of the moulding strip so that there is no chance of the moulding length pivoting slightly on the end of the block.

Type C is usually difficult for the novice until he has had a bit of practice and has the proper feel for positioning the moulding in place. This is the shell and scoop type mouldings

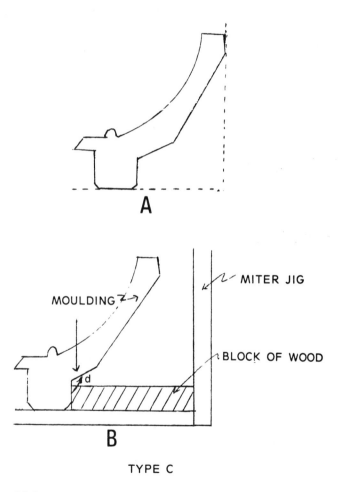

TYPE C

for which, on many professional cutting machines, special jigs are provided. Experience has shown, however, that no special jig is needed if, you will use a bit of patience. If the moulding has been cut as in A so that the base is at right angles to the back of the shoulder, bracing these points against the back and base of the miter jig (or against the bench and the face of the miter guide) when cutting the right end miter will give an accurate cut. If the back of the shoulder is cut at a different angle, however, and this is usually the case, a block as shown in B, will prove sufficient even if the back angle is not 90 deg, provided the base of the moulding is kept flat on the miter jig or bench.

It is seldom that the angle indicated in sketch B of the Type C moulding is a right angle, so it is not advisable to depend on resting this on the block when cutting as it would lift the base out of the flat level position. If you think this is a right angle on any moulding you're using, check it with an accurate try square to make certain.

There is currently a popular moulding pattern which is of the "reverse" style, that is, it slopes outward from the top or front of the shoulder to the base, as indicated by the two profiles below. This type of moulding, which we shall

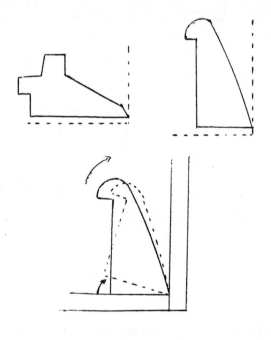

TYPE D

58

designate as Type D, is not difficult to cut if it is not curved or warped, but it is a difficult type to join. It is for this reason that many framers prefer not to use it even though several of the patterns are very handsome and appropriate for capping liners or simple framing of graphics.

As seen previously, so long as the base is held firmly flat on the bench of jig there will be no trouble in cutting. There is a tendency on the part of the inexperienced to tilt the top of the high-style moulding backward, into the position indicated by the dotted lines. As will be obvious, this lifts the base of the moulding and the resulting cut will not be a vertical cut of exactly 45 deg, and proper joining will be impossible even though a less acceptable joint can be made if the tilt was not very great. The primary difficulty with this type of moulding is in the clamping when a corner is joined.

The following diagrams show (A) the result of using clamps in the normal manner with this Type D moulding and (B) how Masonite or cardboard shims should be arranged between the jaws of the clamp and the back or outside of the

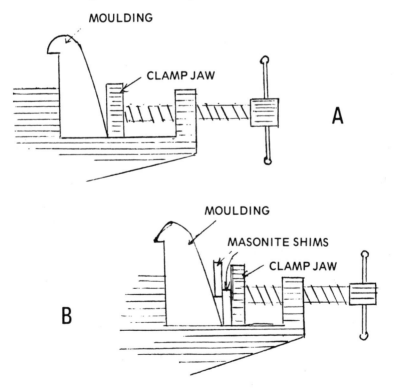

moulding. If the clamp is used without these shims, the fragile beveled edge of the moulding will be crushed in by the required pressure and ruin the appearance of the frame. Use of the shims will put the pressure where it is needed, at the center of the moulding, and will prevent the outer jaw of the clamp from coming into contact with the moulding. If the angle of bevel is very great, as with some flat types of moulding, it might be necessary to use three shims instead of two. In cases of only slight bevel, one shim might serve.

It is advisable to use fairly thick shims, between ⅛ and ¼ inch thick, to avoid being forced to use too many shims for the necessary thickness. Note also that the pressure on these shims is such that they tend to be forced upward and out of the clamps. A hard, slick material for shims is therefore not satisfactory. A soft, rough-surfaced material is best so that it will not mar the moulding or have so little friction that the shims will slide about under pressure.

We have chosen to include a special case of the reverse moulding as Type E because of its somewhat unusual shape and the problem this creates in cutting. This profile, shown in A below, is for a raw, 3-inch oak moulding which is particularly good for use with large seascapes and early American landscapes. A similar type, shown in B, in wormy chestnut 2½ inches wide, presents the same problem and is capable of the same solution. You should note that B is a "reversible" type moulding—one which can be used in two ways. If cut in the manner indicated on the diagram, this will

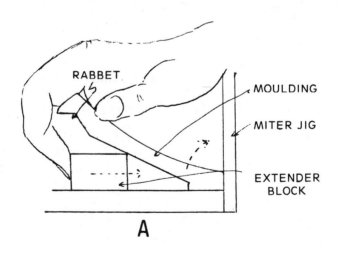

A

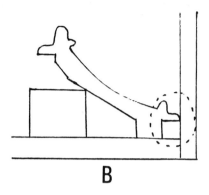

B

TYPE E

give a frame of the reverse type. If, however, the moulding is turned the other way up, making use of the rabbet shown in the dotted circle in B, the resulting frame will be of the "scoop" variety. The versatility of such a moulding makes it popular, but take care that the presence of the two rabbets does not mislead you into making a wrong cut.

In the diagrams A and B, we see that again a block is required for the best stability in handling these mouldings. The block must be held in place with the fingertips with just sufficient firmness to allow the moulding angle to rest on the edge of the block. The pressure is applied against the moulding length itself, backward and downward, to hold the narrow back part in proper position. To place any excess pressure on the auxiliary block in the direction of the straight dashed-line arrow as in A would cause the moulding strip to swing upward, indicated by the curved dashed-line arrow, and result in a cut which could not be joined. You must never forget the **relative** margins of error in framing. That is, a miter cut which is a half-degree or even a full degree off from 45 deg will still provide a sufficiently accurate cut on a half-inch moulding to produce an acceptable joint. On a 3-inch moulding, on the contrary, this error would be so great along the six-times-longer miter cut (equivalent to about ½ inch compared with 3 inches) that the resulting gap would not allow an acceptable joint, if any at all. This is, you recall, the effect of creeping described previously.

Type F, shown below, is a floating moulding, previously discussed. This is a double-rabbeted moulding of which only the inner rabbet is actually designed to hold the painting. In the diagram, sketch A shows how the moulding should be positioned for proper cutting. (For a cross section diagram of

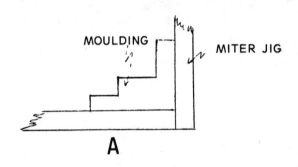

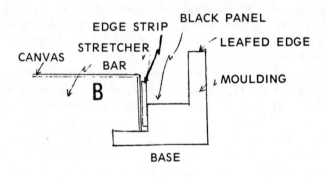

TYPE F

how the painting is set into the moulding, refer to the diagram in the earlier chapter.) The outer edge of the floating moulding is usually finished in a metal leaf, and the panel formed between the edge of the painting and the outer edge is painted black to simulate space. Before mounting an oil in such a floating frame, the edge of the oil stretcher is preferably finished with a thin lath stripping painted black. The floating frame can also be adapted for works under glass if used in conjunction with a conventional rabbeted beading or liner as shown in the following diagram.

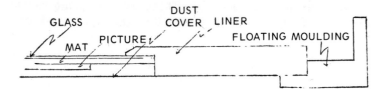

GLASS   DUST
      MAT   PICTURE   COVER   LINER
                 FLOATING MOULDING

One last general type of moulding must be considered. This, which we shall refer to as Type G, is the shadow box or the deep moulding with a double rabbet, both of which are used. This type, mentioned earlier, shown again in profile below, is especially suitable for the framing of objects with a

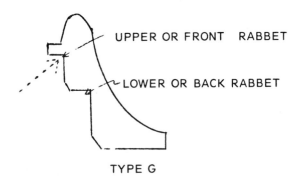

UPPER OR FRONT   RABBET

LOWER OR BACK RABBET

TYPE G

very raised surface, from fans and shells to assemblages of the modern type and old manuscript pages whose cockling render them very difficult if not impossible to be sandwiched in the usual type framing. This is also a fine moulding for giving great depth to a work as the glass is anywhere from ½ to 1 inch in front of the framed work.

If this moulding is to be used as a simple moulding, the upper or outer rabbet indicated by the arrow in the diagram above is the one to be used.

All the above pertains to mouldings which are made for framing and which therefore have the rabbet cut into them. If you wish to use cabinet or construction mouldings for any reason, and from the standpoint of cost they are substantially cheaper, this may be done also. Those who are using bench saws can, if they wish to spend the time and have the necessary skill, cut a rabbet into the moulding themselves. This is not quite so easy in practice as it is in theory, nor is the cutting of moulding patterns a thing to be attempted by a beginner, although it too can be done with combinations of cutting heads. As this book is not intended for such advanced techniques, those who might be interested in such projects are referred to other sources for information.

As for a simple method of providing a rabbet without actually cutting one, see the following illustrations. As shown, the method is simply to cut four strips of wood ⅜ to ½ inch thick and ½ inch wide and to arrange them as at A below.

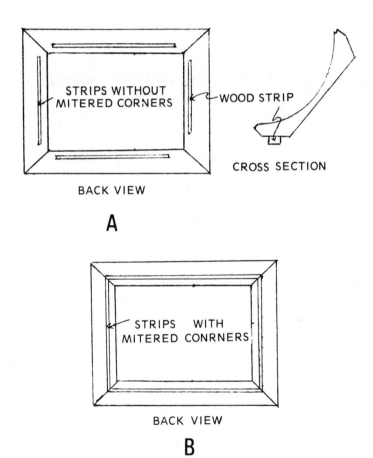

STRIPS WITHOUT MITERED CORNERS

WOOD STRIP

CROSS SECTION

BACK VIEW

A

STRIPS WITH MITERED CONRNERS

BACK VIEW

B

These strips can be nailed or glued to the back of the moulding after the frame has been joined and will serve as rabbeting. If it is an oil or similar original to be mounted in the frame, it will not matter if the corners do not meet, and this will eliminate the need of careful measurement and subsequent mitering.

If the work to be framed is something which must go under glass and therefore needs protection against atmospheric pollution as well as humidity variations, accurate measurements should be made, allowing about ⅜ inch around the inner edge, and the corners must be mitered, as shown in B (left). This substitute rabbeting is something which can be done but which usually takes so much additional time and effort that it is not recommended unless you're forced to it.

Having thus familiarized you with general types of moulding, and having cautioned earlier that there are defects in mouldings which hamper your task, it is time we examine some of the moulding defects and, where possible, suggest corrective measures. We will not consider flaws such as poor-quality finishing, finishes applied over rough or splintered lips and crowns, splits in the moulding, nor patched or filled spots in moulding. If possible, examine the moulding carefully from all sides and angles before buying and refuse any which is inferior quality, since nothing can be done post facto to correct the above faults. Much of the material on sale has not been sufficiently cured for use in framing, and after several months, will begin to warp. Again, there is nothing you can do about this except try to find a reputable supplier who handles only top-quality mouldings. You get what you pay for!

The most common fault in mouldings is **curvature**. This may be in one or both of two directions and is due to either improper storage or to the wood not being sufficiently cured at

TOP VIEW

the time the moulding was cut and finished. Although improper storage can be the cause, this can be corrected by holding the moulding in a proper position for several days to allow it to return to its normal shape. The curving caused by further drying or curing of the wood after the cutting and finishing is impossible to correct or, even if possible, is not practical. The previous diagram shows curvature on the same plane as the moulding whereby the moulding lies flat by the ends curve inward or outward from the true. This is known as "bowing."

The other curvature, shown below, is the type wherein the moulding does not lie flat on its base and, although the ends are in line, they curve up or down from the level. This type of

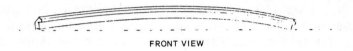

FRONT VIEW

curvature will be referred to as "warping" to differentiate it from bowing.

It is not uncommon to find one or both of these traits in the same length of moulding, frequently in compound form. That is, the bowing may be in both directions producing roughly an S-curve as shown below. This same S-curve is possible in the

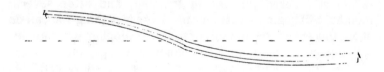

warping as well as in the bowing and, when it comes in both, the result is a corkscrew tendency. Such a length of moulding is beyond salvation and can only be used for some other purpose, if one can be found.

In general, if any aberration occurs in a heavy moulding, it is a matter beyond correction. The time and equipment it would take to correct curvature or twisting in heavy moulding, plus the labor, makes salvage a useless pursuit. The only practical advice we can give is: **get another length of moulding.**

Of course, the correcting of such flaws is based merely on the fact that the moulding must be pliable enough to be bent or twisted in the direction opposite from the flaw. The pattern of the moulding will be a determining factor as well as the type of wood, but in general the size or width of the moulding is the major consideration. The length of the strip is also important as a longer length can be bent a bit more readily than a short one. It will be up to you to make the decision, but a fairly good test is whether or not the straightening can be done in your hands. If so, it will also be possible in the clamps and in fastening the frame to the work.

The flatter, deeper mouldings such as stripping and cappings can be most readily corrected. In every case, you must keep in mind that these mouldings **must be kept straight and level when the miter cuts are made.** This can be very difficult and if any doubt arises, it is better to select another moulding length than to waste time cutting one which seems doubtful for use.

After the cutting, it is first the joints and then the total assembly which must hold the moulding in its proper shape. Let us look first at the effects of curvature on the frame and how this is corrected in the clamps. The diagram below shows (in exaggerated manner) the uncorrected position of mitered

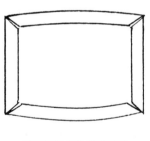

OUTWARD CURVE

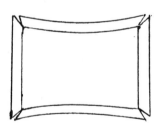

INWARD CURVE

lengths before joining. Note that although the clamps will pull the miters into proper place and straighten the moulding, if the joined corners are not strong enough to overcome the pull of the moulding, the corners will separate again as soon as the clamps are removed. Cross nailing will help strengthen these corners, but the safest and best prevention is, if possible, to put L-plate corner braces at each corner **while the frame is still in the clamps.**

Curvature outward is perhaps more difficult to correct than the inward variety as inward curvature, especially where used to frame oils, is held outward in place by the stretcher bar of the oil. Both types are easier to correct in framing oils, however, as outward curvature can also be corrected by pulling the centers of the moulding strips inward and fastening them with screws or plates to the stretcher bar. If this can be done, there is rarely any need for corner braces or even for cross nailing. This method is illustrated below.

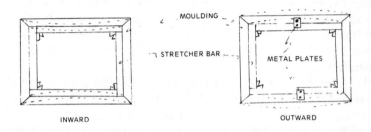

INWARD   OUTWARD

Another frequent defect in moulding is the radial twist, caused by warping along the length of the moulding. This effect, shown below, is the same as if one end of the moulding were held firm while the other end were twisted to the left or

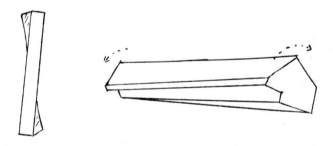

right. This defect, if slight, can easily go undetected in the cutting as the one end can be held properly in place because the other end will turn. It will show up, however, in cutting on the miter jig, as the right-end miter will be held firmly by the stop block and the left end will thus be out of alignment.

If radial twist occurs in minor degree on a thin, narrow capping or similar type pattern, it can be corrected in the joining **provided** it has been held firmly in correct position in the cutting. If this has not been done, there is no way to make a proper joint. Such radial twist, even though it is slight enough to go undetected in the cutting, will produce a frame which is not true and does not lie flat. When such a frame is laid on a flat surface, two diagonal corners will not be level with the other two, allowing the frame to rock on its two lower corners.

This condition may be corrected by holding the frame down flat, using weights on all four sides, and then driving very narrow splines into the **lower** corners (those which, when the frame was laid down, rested on the surface). For this, the frame must be laid **face or front down** and the work done on the back of the corner joints as shown below. As the splines open or spread the alternate corners, the adjoining corners

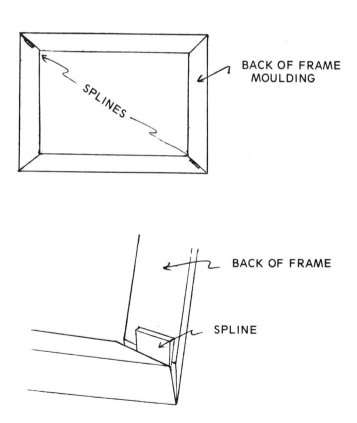

BACK OF FRAME MOULDING

SPLINES

BACK OF FRAME

SPLINE

are forced downward into line with the ones being splined. When the four corners are level, all excess spline can be sanded or planed off to make the back of the frame smooth. It is advisable to add fresh glue to the opened joint and then to reinsert the spline, as this will hold the spline better and give a much stronger joint. If the moulding is small or flat it may be difficult to use a spline which is very long, as the nails would prevent it from being driven in far enough to correct the twist. In such a case, two narrow splines may be used so that they can be driven in between the nails or at either end outside the nails.

Another, fortunately less common, defect in mouldings is the angle of the rabbet being more or less than 90 deg—most commonly more. This presents no problem in cutting, but trying to join the miters properly is a time-consuming effort which seldom is wholly successful. Such a rabbet is shown below, the correct angle being indicated by the dashed line in sketch A. The adjacent diagram (B) shows how a paper match

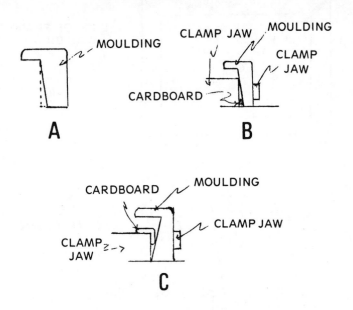

(not match **head**) or bit of cardboard might be inserted between the bottom of the moulding and the jaw of the clamp in order to compensate for the bad cut. If the angle is very slightly off, it is often possible to use a bit of folded paper to provide compensation. If the angle should be less than 90 deg, diagram C shows how to insert a wedge between the upper part of the rabbet and the clamp jaw. This can best be done by folding the paper match over the rim of the clamp jaw, as it is very difficult otherwise to keep it in place. As this is a tedious task when joining, you'd be wiser to check the rabbeting carefully before purchasing any mouldings.

Having thus completed discussion of the pertinent elements concerned with the frame itself, it is time to direct our attention to the next stage in the process of good framing.

SECTION B—
GLASS AND MATS

Tools for Cutting Glass

Tools for cutting glass are few and quite simple. It is possible to use even less tools than we recommended here as we shall see later, but the time spent using makeshift arrangements is not really worth the effort and cost when one considers the ease of using proper tools and the savings in broken glass.

Of prime importance is the glass cutter. There are many on the market. The soundest advice is to spend whatever is necessary for a good cutter and consider that the money will be saved in time and results. The very best cutter is the diamond point. These, however, are too expensive for anyone but the professional framer who is investing in a lifetime tool. Next best is the carbide wheel with bronze bearing. These will cost several dollars, but their superiority over the cheap steel wheel is so great that there is no comparison unless only two or three panes of glass are to be cut. (We shall use the term **pane of glass** as being more readily understood, but the professional designation for a sheet of glass is a **light**.)

A large, steady surface to cut on is a necessity. This should be covered with a soft material which will not scratch the glass. At the same time it must not be so soft that pressure on the glass when cutting can cause irregular breaking. Burlap will serve, but a heavy canvas duck cloth is preferred. A piece of rug with very short nap is also good. The nap must be strong enough so it will not give under pressure. This covering for the cutting board or table must be larger than the glass which is to be cut on it.

A straightedge is indispensable and, although any kind will serve, it is advisable to have either a hard wood or metal edge. The standard professional glazier's square is best, but again it is expensive unless one is going to do a lot of work. For the inexperienced framer or one doing no more than a moderate amount of glass cutting, a wooden T-square is very good provided it is checked to make certain that it is true. These can be purchased at very reasonable prices.

Another advantage of the T-square for cutting is that the end block gives added stability and can be anchored against the edge of the table while the cut is made.

A measuring stick, commonly a yardstick, is required for making measurements and is easier to handle if equipped with an end block to compensate for the thickness of the glass plus that of the T-square. A standard assembly, illustrated below, shows relative positioning for the making of a cut.

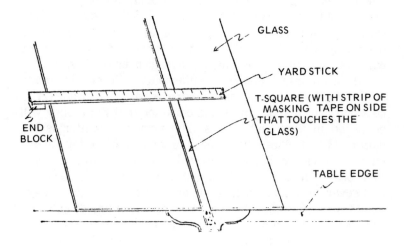

It is possible to use other systems for cutting, such as brads and a straight piece of wood as shown next. A brad is driven into the table on either side of the glass so that the straightedge may be braced against the brads when they are acting as a guide for the cutter. The glass should be positioned so the cut is made along the straightedge opposite to the one against the brads. But this is too tedious a method if much work is being done. It is shown for those who may be cutting only the occasional pane of glass.

Glazier's pliers are excellent for chipping off irregular pieces of glass, if the cut is not clean, but a good pair of square-nose pliers will serve very well, and are generally more available.

Turpentine or kerosene should be available to store the glass cutter in, with enough in a small jar so the wheel and

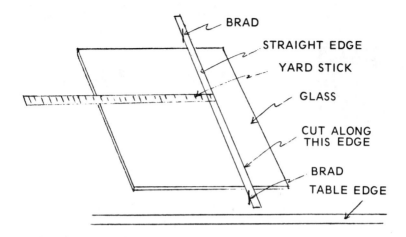

BRAD
STRAIGHT EDGE
YARD STICK
GLASS
CUT ALONG
THIS EDGE
BRAD
TABLE EDGE

axle of the cutter will be covered. Keep the storage jar itself covered. It is best to have a small pad of cloth or felt at the bottom of the jar so that the wheel will not be damaged when it is put into the jar.

Small pieces of cloth are advisable so that they can be used to clean the glass along the line of cutting just prior to making the cut. One of the simplest ways of doing this is to dip the bit of cloth in turpentine and wipe it along the glass. Unless the glass is particularly greasy or dirty, one such application will be sufficient.

Cutting the Glass

The first few attempts at cutting glass are usually disastrous. Either the glass wil not break cleanly along the mark made by the cutter or it suddenly curves away from the line, leaving two odd-shaped pieces. However, don't be discouraged, glass cutting is simple and is purely a matter of technique. Success is the result of practice and of practice only, so the only possible advice is to keep at it until you have achieved the proper feel for the cutter and the glass. This feel comes in a very short time.

Don't waste time practising on those old scraps so often mentioned. They are usually too small to give proper practice and will accustom the hand and wrist to very short cuts—too easy and inadequate for work on larger sizes. After all, few panes for art framing are smaller than 16 x 20 inches, so practice on 8- or 10-inch widths is worse than no preparation at all. Nor is glass so expensive that this economy should be necessary. Most important, however, is the fact that old scraps are old, and old glass is brittle and almost never cuts cleanly, even for experts. It is far better to make the practice cuts on new 20-inch panes even though each costs a few cents more than scrap panes. Once you have become adept at cutting the larger sizes, there is even less problem with the smaller, but certainly the reverse is not true.

Success in cutting glass lies in the use of steady, even pressure for the whole length of the cut and in not allowing the cutter to tilt to either side of vertical at any point. The speed should be moderately fast in making the cut but not so rapid that your hand tends to slide the cutting wheel outward from the line of cut. This happens frequently with beginners, particularly near the beginning of a long cut, and is due to not moving the arm in a direct line but following a natural tendency to let the arm swing outward as it moves back toward the body. (Any one familiar with the stroke in using a billiard or pool cue will readily recognize this tendency.)

As the whole assembly must be immobile in cutting, it is advisable to guard against the possible accidental slip of any of the components. The glass itself will have enough friction against the canvas table cover to remain in place, and the only pressure which should be acting on it is **directly downward.** The T-square or straightedge, whatever is used, should have a strip of masking tape on the bottom side, next to the glass, to prevent the straightedge from slipping sideways either from shift pressure on the hand holding it or sideward pressure as the cutter is drawn along during the cut. If a T-square is used, your hip can help hold it in place against the table edge, just as in cutting mats (discussed later).

When the assembly is properly in place and the glass cleaned along the line of cut, begin the cut just short of the farther or back edge of the glass; otherwise the glass will chip and damage the cutter. Holding the cutter straight and vertical (as shown below) between your fingers, draw the cutter directly **toward your body** along the straightedge or T-square.

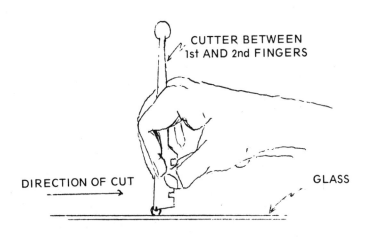

CUTTER BETWEEN
1st AND 2nd FINGERS

DIRECTION OF CUT

GLASS

It takes much less pressure than the beginner supposes to make a good cut. The tendency at first is to press too hard. This is not only unnecessary, it gives a bad cut which is far more difficult to handle. Usually the pressure at the beginning is correct and then, as the hand and wrist approach the body and the end of the cut, you will unconsciously increase pressure. This is natural also as the arm is no longer extended to weaken the pressure.

A cut with too much pressure will produce small chips or flakes along the line of cut. This does not produce a clean cut and increases the chances of the glass breaking away in a curve from the main line of cut.

As soon as the cut has been made, shift the glass so the end extends a couple of inches over the table edge and tap the glass gently but firmly **on the under side beneath the cut** with the end of the cutter handle. The tap should be directly under the cut and should not be made with the end of the cutter handle. The tap should be directly under the cut and should not be made with any cutter which has a sharp, small end, as this generally tends to cause a star type break and ruin the sheet of glass. This tap will have to vary with the thickness of the glass and comes also only as a result of practice. In general, the thicker the glass, the sharper and harder the tap. Photo glass breaks very easily, picture glass less so. The nonreflecting types and single-weight commercial glass take a much more forceful tap.

Then place a pencil or the handle of the cutter under the glass directly under the cut and parallel to it, lengthwise, and apply pressure with both hands downward on both sides of the cut. The glass should snap easily and cleanly along the line of cut.

A matchstick is often suggested as the fulcrum to put under the glass to break it, even by manufacturers of the cutters. Our experience has been that this is sufficient for only quite small panes of glass and that a larger object such as a pencil is best for all uses.

When cutting a narrow strip off one end of a pane of glass, and as little as a ¼ inch or even less can be taken off quite easily, it is not possible to use the pencil or matchstick as a fulcrum. After tapping the glass, turn the pane so the edge to be discarded is over the table edge. Then use either your fingers or pliers to make the break. A clean snap is needed for this. If an inch or more is to be cut off, fingers are recommended. If the strip is smaller, either glazier's pliers or the square-nose pliers mentioned earlier are required.

There is often a slight curve at one end or the other away from the cut. This is broken off with the pliers without difficulty. If the amount is very small, too small for the jaws to grip and work in a downward break, you must resort to the technique of gnawing or skinning. In this method, the jaws of the pliers are tightened gently on the glass and the pliers drawn away from the edge. This results in a rapid, chipping action by the plier jaws and will quickly remove the excess glass. The same technique is used for small edges and shards which have not cut cleanly away.

Do not leave glass sit for any length of time between the cut and the break. Glass should be tapped and broken immediately after the cutter has been used. To delay increases the possibility of ruining the glass.

Do not cut over a previous cut nor across a cut. This is bad for the cutting wheel, of course, but worst of all it will almost always lead to breakage.

It is sometimes advisable to turn the glass around after the cutter has marked the glass and to tap the beginning of the cut rather than the end. This is often helpful for novices since, as mentioned earlier, there is a tendency for the beginning of the cut to be cleaner and lighter than the end. A good mark by the wheel will be hardly more than a hairline across the glass. Anything wider or deeper is too much.

Although few people will be cutting ovals or circles, it is sometimes necessary or desirable to do so. Just as there are machines for cutting straight edges on glass, so are there special machines for cutting ovals and circles—circles being just a special case of the oval. These are seldom found, even among professional framers, since the oval style is not so popular as it once was. If an oval or circle is desired, however, the simplest and best practice is to have it cut by a professional. For those who wish to cut their own, the following section will be helpful.

First of all, the cut will be freehand. Cutting around a template or model is very difficult, and, because it induces a very uneven pressure, tends to cause more difficulty than freehand cutting.

Many of the old oval and round frames had very wide rabbeting, in some cases fully an inch. If this is the case, it is possible to fit a glass without going through the difficulties of cutting the oval or round at all. As shown below, the glass can be made to fit just by cutting off corners, either with four or eight cuts.

When this is not practical, a slower system must be relied on. Those familiar with geometry will recall a system for

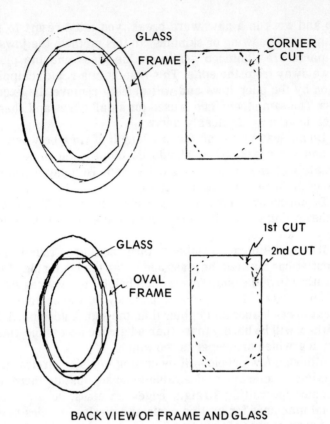

GLASS

FRAME

CORNER CUT

GLASS

OVAL FRAME

1st CUT

2nd CUT

BACK VIEW OF FRAME AND GLASS

drawing ovals by use of two pegs and a length of string **longer** than the distance between the two pegs. For very accurate work such a system is fine, but it is really not needed. So long as the frame is available, the easiest and most practical system is to trace through the opening in the frame with a pencil onto a sheet of white paper. This will give the oval shape opening, but one smaller than the true opening because of the width of the pencil. This tracing is shown below. The dashed

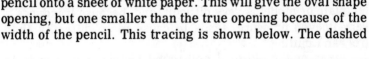

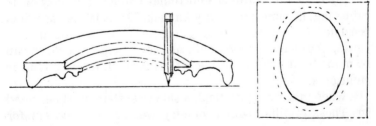

lines indicate the additional amount which must be added all around, since **the glass must fit the rabbet in the back of the frame.** The tracing with pencil was to give the correct shape of the opening.

With the pencil or a pen, make the outer line (the dashed line) continuous and dark so that it can be seen very easily. Place this outline on the glass-cutting table, drawing up, and lay a pane of glass over it. Holding the glass and drawing down firmly with one hand, take the cutter in the other and slowly, steadily follow the pencil line with the cutting wheel, making cut lines as indicated below. After making an arc of one-fourth of the oval (one-sixth if the glass is large), guide the cutting

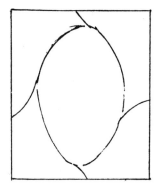

wheel **almost** to the outer edge. Then return to the point of departure and begin the cut for the next section. For the sake of clarity, the diagram does not show the lines as touching. However, the lines should touch each other to make the cut clean and reduce the chance of a bad break. When all the cuts have been made, tap the glass along all the lines enough to begin cleavage. Then carefully use your fingers to break off first one section and then the next. When all the sections have been broken loose, use pliers to pull off any points left where the cuts met.

Before using any glass, check it for defects. Many pieces, even though they are purchased in cases, have scratches or scrapes across the surface due to careless handling. Occasionally there are bits of imbedded dirt, and long flaws which distort the picture are quite common. From time to time you'll see glass with small bubbles. While many of these are considered within allowable specifications by the manufacturer and controlling agencies, don't buy them for framing. These flaws will spoil a picture, so glass containing any visible flaws should never be used.

The better quality the glass, of course, the less chance of flaws, as requirements are more stringent and quality control is better. The best quality glass currently available is called **photo glass**. It is thin and very free of defects. The next best, known as **picture glass**, is the type most commonly used by picture framers. It is somewhat heavier than photo glass and, as a result, can be used for larger sizes. The next type generally available is the **single weight**, a type frequently used for fine cabinetwork in doors and one used in general construction. This comes in large sizes and should be the lowest quality even considered for frames.

The more recent nonglare or nonreflecting glass comes in only one thickness and one grade, though in many sizes. This is considerably more expensive than the regular glass per square foot. If you wish to use this, buy a size which gives the minimum waste. The glass itself is more difficult to cut than regular glass as it is heavier and, in practice, tends more to break away from the cut line when fractured. Since the surface is rougher than regular glass it does take the mark of the wheel more easily and in this respect is much easier to handle without slippage of the wheel or curving when making the cut.

Tools for Cutting Mats

Since mats are used so frequently in commercial art as well as by art students and professional artists, there are many tools available for cutting them. This includes machines for cutting oval and circular openings as well as electrically driven cutters. As before, we will assume that you are not doing production framing and will not be interested in the expensive machinery available.

As with glass cutting, the basic tools are a cutter and a straightedge. The cutter is a mat knife, a handle which holds replaceable blades of very sharp steel. Paper dulls a cutting edge very rapidly, so be especially careful to change blades frequently. Once again, the cost of blades is negligible compared with the cost of matboard or the disappointment of a messy job.

There are several types of cutter-and-straightedge combinations available in the inexpensive category, but these are less suitable for the nonprofessional than might be supposed. Almost every type provides a system for beveling the edge of the mat, but they are not so easy to manipulate as you might be led to believe. There are also adjustable blade cutters which are to be used in conjunction with a straightedge. For those who wish to use them, and who have had some experience using them, they are fine. The chief disadvantage to them, considered rather serious by many professionals, is that the blade must go **completely through** the matboard in making the cut, even a bit into the covering surface of the cutting table.

This means that instead of making the cut in several repeated strokes, you must cut through the total thickness of the matboard in one stroke. Anyone who has attempted to cut a line through even thin cardboard in one stroke will appreciate the difficulty. In addition, the great force needed to push the knife blade along through the matboard frequently causes the board and cutting assembly to slip, thus ruining the mat. It is, however, a matter of personal choice as to what type of cutter is used.

As in the cutting of glass, a level and solid surface is required. If a table is used which has a crack or any toughness on it, it should be covered with a sheet of Masonite or similar material to provide a smooth surface. This will serve as the surface also to cut on, although many framers prefer to use a layer of craftboard or cardboard over that. The covering, no matter what it is, must be securely fastened so it will not slide.

A good, steel T-square is the most versatile item for guiding the mat knife. The T-square base should be deep enough so that it will fit well down over the edge of the table, and this edge should be straight and smooth.

A yardstick or other measuring device is necessary. Most inexpensive items vary a bit in the calibration due to width of marks and so forth, so it is best to use the same item for measuring the mat as is used in measuring the other components, such as work to be framed and margins, as well as the rabbet measurement of the frame. This will insure consistency or precision of work no matter how inaccurate the yardstick may actually be.

For cutting, we prefer and recommend the thick-handled mat knife with the wide, sturdy blade. It is much easier to handle than the narrow ones and gives a surer grip. It is also less tiring on the hand when much matting is to be done and provides better control if beveling of the mat is desired.

A pencil, medium grade, seems to be best for marking the matting as it gives a readily visible line without being unduly difficult to clean off. Hard pencils, especially if sharpened to a fine point, tend to press into the mat. This makes a depressed line which cannot be removed. This is no problem, if back cutting is done but it spoils the mat when one is cutting from the front.

A good, soft eraser is recommended for cleaning the mat.

Very fine sandpaper is sometimes useful for cleaning off the burring along the edge of the mat if the cut should be a little ragged due to a dull blade or defaced surface under the mat.

"Boning," the technique of going over a cut edge with a type of burnisher to smooth out the raised effect caused by cutting, is usually done by professionals with a smoothly rounded bit of bone or other hard material or an agate burnisher. In general, the same thing can be accomplished with the handle of the mat knife, if it is rounded, or even with the thumbnail.

Cutting the Mats

No matter whether the mat is cut from the front or the back, the object is to achieve a straight, clean cut with sharp corners. For this it is essential to have a good cutting surface, a sharp blade and practiced, steady technique. We will discuss numerous matting techniques in this chapter, but it is not available for the beginner to attempt them until he has become adept at cutting the simple mat. Nothing will do as much to ruin a beautiful picture as a sloppy mat around it. Conversely, a crisp, clean mat job will enhance any picture.

The theory of mat cutting is simple. You determine the size of the picture you wish to mat or to mat and frame. Then measure the rabbet of the frame, or measure the outer size of the mat decided on if only matting is desired. This, when marked out on the matboard, produces a hollow rectangle as shown below. Standard sizes for matboard run 30 x 40 inches although smaller and larger are available depending on the manufacturer and the type of matboard. Fancy mats, such as grasscloth-covered or fabric-covered of any kind, tend to run

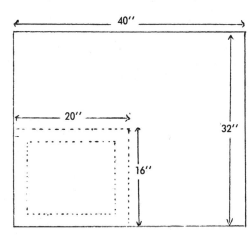

2" WIDE MAT

in smaller sizes but greater cost per sheet. It is customary when making a simple mat to cut the outer size first from the large sheet and then to cut out the center to make the requisite mat.

In cutting the outer edges, or basic mat section, lay the sheet of matboard on the table, preferably face up, and place the T-square at the proper position. The fundamental rule of mat cutting is **ALWAYS HAVE THE UNWANTED PART OF THE MAT WHERE THE KNIFE WILL GO INTO THAT IN CASE OF A SLIP.** Looking at the diagram below, the reasoning behind this will be clear. If we wish to cut a mat

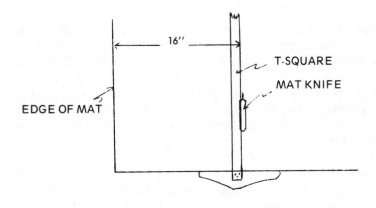

whose outer dimensions are 16 x 20, we measure 16 inches from the left edge of the sheet to the **right edge** of the T-square. The blade of the knife, for a right-handed framer, will then be **outside** the area desired. If for any reason the knife should slip, it will go into the area to the right of the T-square where, although it may ruin a section of the matboard, it will not ruin the section which is to be used. (Of course, this will be reversed for a left-handed framer who would be measuring from the righthand edge of the board and cutting on the lefthand edge of the T-square.) Whether cutting the **blank**, as this basic piece of mat is called, or cutting out the **window** or unwanted inner portion, this same rule must be applied. Even experienced mat cutters have been known to make slips of the knife. Some cutters use a strip of masking tape or cloth tape on the bottom surface of the T-square to give added grip against slipping, but this is more a precaution than a necessity. Use the fingertips of the free hand, not the hand used in cutting, to press firmly down on the blade of the T-square. There is quite a bit of flexibility, even in the steel and magnesium T-squares, unless they have a thick or a moulded blade.

A good trick to learn is that of making a downward punch with the tip of the mat knife when beginning and especially when ending the cut. This is done by positioning the tip of the knife at the top or farthest end of the line at a more vertical angle than for the cutting and then pressing downward to more or less stab the matboard. Do **not** push all the way through. Then, slanting the knife back to the proper cutting angle, which should not be too much off the vertical, bring the knife smoothly and quite rapidly **toward your body** along the edge of the T-square. Stop just short of the end of the line at the bottom or near edge. Without lifting the mat knife off the board, tilt it slightly more toward the vertical again and punch downward slightly. The purpose of this is to make a pit in the matboard at the beginning and end of the cut. It makes it easier to place the knife blade in exactly the same spot at the top when beginning the cut, and if your cutting speed at the end is slower than at the beginning, it allows the tip of the knife to drop into the little pit and prevent overcutting. One of the greatest causes of unsightly mats is the overcut corner, where the cutter has gone beyond the proper junction point.

The pitting at the beginning and end of the line to be cut is not necessary when cutting the outer dimensions, especially at the near edge where the cut will run off the edge of the matboard, but it is still a good idea to use it at the beginning of the cut even when just cutting the blank from a larger sheet.

Some matboards are tougher than others and require more strokes of the mat knife to cut them. Rather than to apply more pressure in the case of tougher board, it is better to maintain your usual pressure and merely make more cuts. **Consistency is the framer's friend.**

The following figure shows the three possible ways of treating the angle of cut when cutting matboard. The straight edge in A is seldom desirable as it is neither an outward bevel nor does it hide the center, pulp portion, of the matboard. If an unbeveled effect is desired, the knife and blade should be canted **outward** from the edge of the T-square to give the effect shown in B. This slight undercutting or reverse bevel allows the colored or facing surface to hide the ⅛ inch or so of uncolored pulp which comprises most of the mat's thickness.

In C, we have the regular bevel. This is usually less than 45 deg and is formed by canting the cutting blade **inward**, leaning

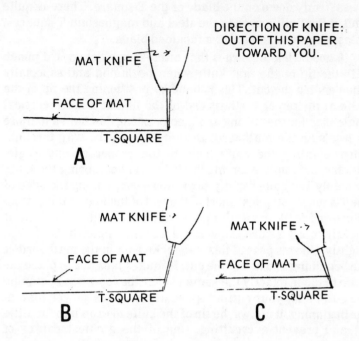

DIRECTION OF KNIFE:
OUT OF THIS PAPER
TOWARD YOU.

over the blade of the T-square. In some of the devices on the market for cutting mats, the blade angle is adjustable in the holder and can be set for a definite angle. In freehand cutting, it will be up to your skill in positioning for the angle. In cutting the bevel, good technique is extremely important as **the blade must follow the same angle each time a cut is made.** Otherwise the cut will be "layered" from the blade cutting at different angles and will make the mat unsightly. Back cutting, which we shall discuss shortly, is helpful in the cutting of bevels as you can use your fingertips as a guide and, with practice, you can cut clean bevels at will.

As mentioned earlier, there are two ways of cutting mat, either from the front or from the back. Front cutting has the advantage of insuring sharper front edges though there is greater risk of soiling the mat or cutting beyond the proper point at the corner. It is the better system to use when cutting a fabric-covered matting, and if care is taken it will not cause any more soiling than cutting from the back.

There are cases, however, when the mat **must** be cut **from the back.** Some surfaces are so delicate and prone to finger marks, or else have a textured surface from which pencil marks cannot be successfully removed, that cutting from the back is the only way to achieve a neat result. In addition, dark colored and black mats are very difficult to work with from the face as guiding lines will not show up easily. Since the back of matboards is either white or off-white, it is always easy to see the pencil marks on the back. Note in the following discussion that the two procedures require the reversal of instructions regarding positioning of tools and of tilting or canting of the cutting blade. As we shall see later, it is almost mandatory that back cutting be used when multiple-matting is desired.

When cutting from the front, as little marking is used as is necessary since the mat face will have to be cleaned afterward. In cutting from the back, no such consideration is necessary. Consequently, the markings are usually run from one edge to the other. In the figure below, A shows a typical marking for the face or front cut while B shows the customary method of marking for the back cut.

In the following diagram, the difference in direction of canting the knife is shown in cutting a bevel.

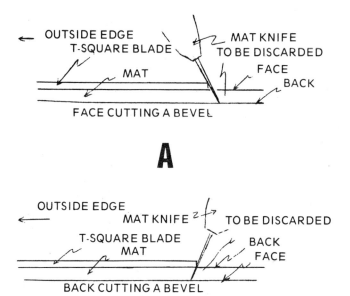

The corner is most frequently the downfall of the non-professional mat cutter, so pay special attention to it. It is frequently preferred to stop just short of the corner in making the cuts and then, when the four side cuts have been made, finish cutting the corners freehand, using slow pressure of the knife to release the corners. Some cutters use a razor blade for this but it isn't necessary if the blade of the mat knife is sharp (as it should be). Take care in releasing the corners to keep the same line and bevel as the side cut. If this is not done, an unsightly indentation about ¼ inch long will be the result, as indicated in the figure below. This or any other curve or indentation in the edge of the mat is almost impossible to trim away again and usually the mat has to be recut.

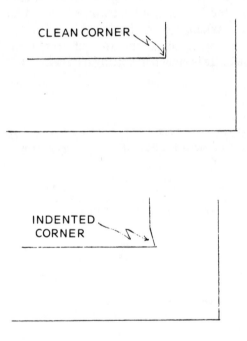

It is perhaps not so obvious that the cutting of corners is a bit easier with the back cut than with front cutting, due to the angle of the knife blade. In back cutting, the top of the knife angles toward the cutter. This means that you can go **slightly** beyond the juncture point as shown by the lines when cutting, because the tip of the blade is about ⅛ inch behind the portion of the blade visible at the level of the back of the mat. If carefully done, cutting from the back permits the corner to be cut out cleanly without further trimming.

If in the cutting, from whichever direction, the bottom of the board rests on a previous cut or flaw or if the knife blade is dulled from excessive use, a "burr" will be caused along the edge of the mat, as shown below. If this is on the **face** of the mat, it should be rubbed down with a burnisher 'bone' or the

BONE IN THIS DIRECTION   BURRED EDGE

thumbnail in the direction **opposite** to the lifting so the little tears or wrinkles will be ironed down again. If on the **back** edge of the mat, or if the burnishing leaves small, ragged edges, a piece of very fine sandpaper brushed carefully along the edge with a slight downward motion **toward the other surface** of the matboard will usually correct the burr.

Cutting oval or circular mats pose nearly the same problems as cutting oval or circular glasses. The circular forms are, of course, quite easy to lay out as they may be accurately drawn by means of a compass, whether one is working with glass or with mats. As we have discussed in the section on cutting glass, the oval is a difficult form to reproduce without the professional machine for cutting mats and glass in oval forms.

It is exceedingly difficult for even the practiced professional to cut a clean oval or circle freehand, and practically impossible for the nonprofessional. Matboard requires a steady, smooth cutting to give clean edges, something impossible to accomplish freehand, although the skilled professional can render a good approximation. The only advice which we can give you is to cut **carefully**, resting the heel of your free hand on the inner portion of the oval. Do not try to cut completely through the mat in one stroke, but cut completely through in several strokes before moving along to the next small section. The little imperfections in the arc can be smoothed out to a large extent by judicious use of very fine sandpaper.

9 Mat Variations

The use of mats in framing is somewhat of an art within an art. So much can be accomplished by proper use of mats that any time spent experimenting with effects is well worthwhile. We will not concern ourselves with matting from an aesthetic standpoint in this book insofar as this would involve color harmonics and balance, nor will we attempt any discussion of the proper relationships among frame moulding, work framed, and matting. The scope here will be limited to what may be done to prepare mats in the process of framing.

It will be best to start with the single mat, cut from a larger piece. As we have seen, this may have the straight edge (with slight reverse bevel) or a definite, intentional bevel of noticeable width. What can be done with this?

First, it may be left just as it is. In some cases with white matting, this off-white bevel makes a very pleasing demarcation strip between mat and picture and is very desirable. In other cases, where the picture may have dark border areas but a dark mat is desired, this bevel will serve to separate the two and prevent the mat from merging with the picture area. As mentioned earlier, the center portion of the matboard is an off-white.

In other cases, it may prove advantageous to color the bevel, providing a sort of fillet. One of the common (and very much favored in former eras) ways of doing this is to coat it with a bronze or gold paint. The gold is quite neutral, providing a brightness around the picture area, and will go with almost any work.

Other colors may also be applied, either to supplement the mat color or to provide a contrast. This is especially true where you may have used a thick matboard or a craftboard, perhaps ¼ inch thick, where the bevel is deep and therefore of great importance in the overall effect. One of the easiest ways to color such a bevel is with the popular marking crayon which uses a form of colored ink or dye. Care must be observed with them (as with any other medium) to make certain the colored ink or dye does not "bleed" into the mat face and discolor it along the edge.

The modern polymer colors are also satisfactory for this, provided you are careful to keep the water content as little as possible, lest it soak the mat. The same advice holds for the casein paints and watercolors which are also popular for

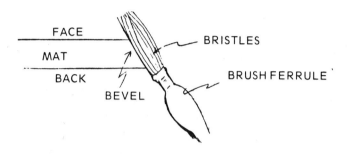

coloring bevels. The diagram above shows how the brush should be held in applying these colors. A filbert-shaped or flat brush should be used and the **side** of the bristles applied to the edge. Use of the end of the brush would cause separate bristles to spread over the edge limit and put unwanted color on the mat.

Pastel pencils and crayons are also used for coloring the bevel, but they are less recommended than the others.

In addition to the coloring of the bevel, lines may be put on the mat face around the picture opening to add interest, break up the flat area, or add a bit of color. These are called "French lines" and are commonly found only on single mats though they may be used if needed on the multiple mats. They are usually ruled in, using a T-square for guidance.

The French line has variations which have been more used in the past than in contemporary times, but it is a very effective addition to a mat or picture if properly handled and not overdone. The following figures show a mat with one line (A), with two lines (B), and with three lines (C). The lines may vary in thickness, the center one of three being twice as wide as the outer lines, or one line may be discontinuous as in C either dashes or dots.

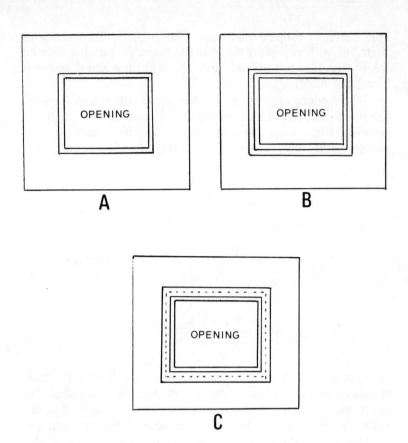

The lines, if more than one, are often of different colors to enhance the effect, perhaps one brown, the next red, and the outermost, black. You will profit greatly by experimenting with such combinations.

In addition to these variations, it is possible to color the area between two lines. This was immensely popular in the 1800s in England, one of the favorite combinations being one gold line with two deep red lines having a rose color in between. The shaded area in the following diagram gives an idea of the effect. Such tinting of area was and is usually done with watercolor, as the transparent nature of the medium gives a lovely, delicate effect. Great care must be taken in doing such work and it is well to rest your hand on the blade of the T-square to provide steadiness and guidance to the hand and wrist.

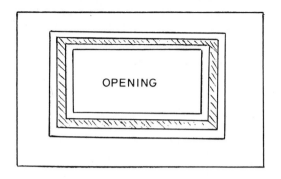

Sometimes wider strips of paper such as gold foil are cut to size and glued around the picture opening some distance away from it, as shown below. The end of the paper strips should be very carefully matched if this is done and the center of the line marked in pencil to help guide in the laying in of the strips.

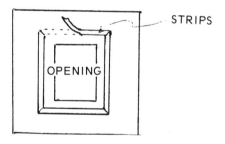

In putting in lines, the most successful system is to mark the lines in very carefully first in pencil. Then draw the ink line over this, and when the ink is completely dry, erase the overlapping pencil lines at the corners with a gum eraser. Of course, if the ink line is slightly off the pencil line, that pencil line should also be erased.

Black or dark lines are occasionally used on color mats— so are contrasting white or light ones. In general, however, a colored mat is by itself so strong in effect that French lines are inappropriate. The French line is best used for white or off-white or very pastel shade mats. When more color or sparkle is needed in conjunction with a colored mat, it is customary and best to add another mat to form a narrow band of **fillet** around the picture. This, in effect a double mat, will be covered later in the discussion of multiple mats.

Anything which will make a line is usable for making the French line, and there is at least one commercial gadget on the market which is a combination edge guide, wheel, and ink reservoir so that lines of varied thickness, either continuous or broken, may be rolled onto the mat. In general, however, the professional framer uses the draftsman's inking or lettering pens for this work and these are recommended even though the inexperienced will have to practice a bit with them.

For just occasional work for the nonprofessional, and for much of the advanced work, ballpoint pens are perfectly satisfactory. First, they are cheap, and if ruined by rubbing against the T-square, can be easily replaced. Second, they do not pose the same problem of dropping ink blobs or at least so much ink that it will smear when the T-square is shifted or lifted. On the other hand, they do **not** dry instantaneously and thus, will smear if rubbed to soon after inking. Third, they come in a variety of colors.

The worst failing of the ballpoint pen in making French lines is that the colors tend to fade, some more rapidly than others. However, many of the current watercolors are aniline dyes which will fade equally quickly. The other disadvantage of the ballpoint for this work is its tendency to gum or clog up from the microscopic bit of lint and paper scraped from the surface as a line is being made. For this and other reasons, including less precision of manufacture in the cheaper types, the ballpoint will frequently begin a line and then suddenly blank out, perhaps to begin marking the line again further along. In such cases, the line is not only a skip but is almost invariably of different widths. Be careful in using the ballpoint that the line has been made continuously and of equal width all along. If not, immediately begin at the beginning and remark over the line, varying pressure if need be in order to make the line of equal width at all points.

In making French lines with a ballpoint, wipe the point off carefully after each line. Otherwise the accumulation of lint or paper on the ball will cause a thick and fuzzy line the next time it is used.

At times, especially when a simple moulding is used to set off an ornate picture, the French line is placed ½ to ¾ inch away from the **moulding** edge to bring more emphasis to the outer portion of the frame and balance the effect of the picture framed.

It was mentioned earlier that if additional color is wanted when using mats, it is customary to add a fillet of color by using another mat. This is one example of multiple matting and probably the most commonly used one. It is done in the following manner: First, the outer or capping mat is cut to the proper dimensions except that the **window is cut larger** to allow for the addition of the fillet. This fillet can be any width, but less than 1⁄16 inch is difficult to cut and too narrow to be visible, in short, inadequate, and anything over 3⁄8 inch is too obtrusive. Normally, the fillet is 1⁄8 to 1⁄4 inch wide. Whatever the width of the fillet, this must be taken into account when cutting out the inner opening or window in the capping mat. Do not forget that in addition to the amount of mat needed to fit into the rabbet, allowance must also be made for the **overlap** of the mat into the picture area.

It is well at this point to discuss a concrete example so that the relationships may become quite clear. Assuming ⅛ inch fillet of white to offset a brown overmat where the picture area is 16 x 20 inches and a total of 3 inches of matting is to be **visible**, the diagram below will be helpful in following the discussion and understanding the reasoning for the variations

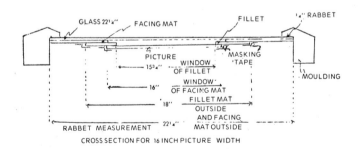

CROSS SECTION FOR 16 INCH PICTURE WIDTH

in the measurements. If the matting overlaps the picture on all sides a depth of ⅛ inch, necessary so that the picture can be properly fastened to the back of the mat, the dimensions are easily calculated.

The width would be 15¾ inches plus 6 inches for **both** sides of the mat plus ½ inch to allow for the two rabbet depths, for a total of 22¼ inches. The height would be 19¾ inches plus the same 6½ inches, for a total of 26¼ inches. Now, normally the window cut into the mat, if it's a single mat, would be 15¾ inches by 19¾ inches to allow for overlapping of the picture. This will now become the **inner** measurement or window of the fillet. The outer edge of the fillet mat will be this plus 1⅛ inches on each side so that the fillet can be mounted to the facing or capping mat. Thus the fillet mat will measure 15¾ plus 2¼ or 18 inches wide and 19¾ plus 2¼ or 22 inches high.

The facing or outer mat will have a 16 x 20 window, allowing ⅛ inch fillet to be visible on all sides and be the rabbet measurement at the outer dimension on the outside— 22¼ x 26¼ inches.

The previous diagram shows how this looks in cross section when assembled. Note particularly that masking tape is used to secure the fillet mat to the facing mat and the picture to the fillet. Masking tape is used because it holds securely, yet, if need be, it may be removed with minimum damage to either the back of the picture or to the back of the matting. For this reason, masking tape is far preferable to a glue or rubber cement.

It is often desired in professional or fine art framing to utilize more than a mat with fillet. For example, many works look better if **three** mats are used. A brown-green-black composition on an off-white background may look much better with a brown facing mat, a ¼ inch white filleting next to that, and a ⅛ inch black fillet adjacent to the picture. The same procedure is followed as before, the only difference being that this time an **additional** fillet must be taken into account. Using the same example as before, the 16 x 20 with 3 inches total mat to show, the measurements would be computed thus: 15¾ plus ¼ (i.e., twice the ⅛ inch black fillet) plus ½ (twice the ¼ inch white fillet) plus ½ (twice the ¼ inch rabbet) plus 5¼ (twice the width of the brown mat necessary to make the visible 3 inches of matting desired). This latter computation is most easily arrived at by computing 3 inches **minus** the ¼ inch white fillet **minus** the ⅛ inch black fillet, or 3 inches minus ⅜ inch leaves 2⅝ inches as the width of **one** side of the brown mat. This must be doubled when figuring the **total width** of the mat. In this case, the total width of the brown mat would be 22¼ inches as before and the height 26¼ inches as before.

But note the difference: With the two-mat arrangement, the visible width of the brown mat is 3 inches **minus** ⅛ inch fillet, or 2⅞ inches. With the three mats, to allow two fillets, the visible width of the brown mat is 3 inches minus ⅛ minus ¼ for a total width of 2⅝ inches. If the brown is to be kept wider, say the full 3 inches, then the frame must be made larger to compensate. It is for this reason particularly that the matting must be carefully considered before the frame is made!

It should be mentioned that differences of ⅛ inch or so in outer mat width will not be noticeable. However, differences of only 1/16 or even less are quite noticeable on the filleting. Especially will these be noted if, say, just one side is slightly thicker than the others. Hence the extreme care required in cutting the windows when filleting is used.

It is because of this need for great accuracy when using fillet mats that it is better to do such cutting from the **back** of the matboard. It is so often necessary to mark a line again or to compensate for any slight differences in making the measurements that trying to clean the face of the mat would result in messy erasures which could never be completely eradicated. By utilizing the back-cutting method, centering the larger window opening over the tentatively marked back will soon show if the measurements are too large, too small, or not even for the height and width fillets. The dotted lines below show the window of the facing mat placed over the marks for

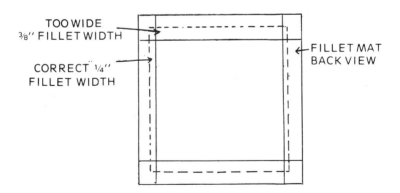

the window of the white fillet mat. Note that the top and bottom fillets are too wide compared to the side fillets. Thus, the back of the white mat would have to be remeasured and remarked so that all filleting is equal. If the top and bottom are too generous and give fillets more than ¼ inch while the sides are too meager and give fillets less than ¼ inch, it is preferable to remeasure the whole thing. Otherwise, merely correct the sides which are off.

For this, it is usually easier to trim off from just one side. Suppose that both top and bottom fillets were 1/16 inch too wide. Rather than try to cut 1/16 off each, trim 1/8 inch off just one end. The mat can then be centered so that the filleting is proper all around. The difference in position will make no difference to the appearance of the matting when viewed from the front.

This same trial and error system will be used again for the black fillet, only this time it is the white filleting mat and its window which will be measured against the black mat, with any corresponding changes made in the marking for the window of the black mat.

From the previous illustration, it should be apparent that the outer or facing mat should be cut first. For the cutting of the white fillet mat, measure the **inside dimensions** of the brown facing mat and add 2 inches to each. This will provide 1 inch on all sides for fastening to the back of the brown mat.

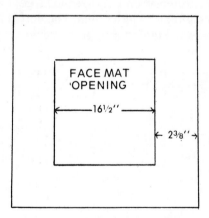

FACE MAT
OPENING

16½"

2⅜"

Now, measure carefully **one and one-quarter inches** in from each edge and make the line. If accurately done, this will give a window just ¼ inch smaller all around than the window in the brown mat, as shown below. If the brown mat is placed over this and the lines do not show that a fillet of ¼ inch will

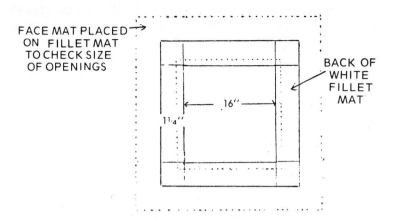

FACE MAT PLACED ON FILLET MAT TO CHECK SIZE OF OPENINGS

BACK OF WHITE FILLET MAT

16"

1¼"

show all around, remark the lines so that the proper width is achieved. Cut this window out and then repeat the procedure for the black mat—making certain that on this one there is only **one and one-eighth inches** measured in from the outer edge as only a ⅛ inch fillet of black is required.

When all is finished, the black fillet mat when placed over the picture should overlap it ⅛ inch on all sides. If the cutting is made without reference to this, there is a chance that the window in the black fillet will be either too large, which cannot be corrected and another will have to be cut, or too small. If too small, it will overlap a bit too much. This may be left as is or a bit trimmed from the black to reduce the size of the fillet. It is wise, therefore, beginning with the white fillet, to make measurements to be sure the mat windows are close to what they should be. Small factors, including the width of the distance between pencil point and T-square blade, make variations which can accumulate to an unbelievable degree. **By checking each step as you go along**, you can avoid difficulty at the end and possible ruining of the whole mat job.

While it is possible to do this same matting in other ways, the method above seems to produce the best results and simplify the skill and accuracy required. For the non-professional, it is without doubt the one to use. It may seem easier to the beginner to make the black fillet to fit the picture area as desired, then to cut the white fillet mat, and, last, the brown facing mat. In practice, the care required in measuring and the calculations necessary in computing the dimensions for the next mat make this far more difficult than the system we suggested. There is no reason why the latter system cannot be used, however, if you find it more suited to your temperament and technique.

One other type of mat that we developed has proven of excellent use in fine art framing. This is known as the "split" mat because it is essentially a facing mat cut into two sections and arranged on a backing mat of different color to give a three-dimensional effect with **both French line and fillet elements.** A cross section of the double mat is shown below.

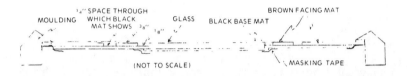

Making the split type mat is not difficult, but extreme care is needed in the cutting as the inner strip is very fragile to handle and will easily twist or tear. Assume, as in the diagram, that we are going to use a black mat next to the picture with a brown overlay or face mat.

First cut the black mat 1 inch smaller than the proper rabbet size and with the window to fit the picture area. Then cut the brown mat the exact rabbet size with a window ¼ inch larger than the black mat. This will allow a fillet of ⅛ inch all around. Stop! Do not attach the mats yet.

Measuring back from the edge of the window in the brown mat, measure off ⅜ inch and ⅝ inch all around and draw in the lines. First cut out the strip indicated by the ⅜ inch mark and save it carefully. This four-sided piece will later be glued to the black mat. Now cut away the piece marked out at the ⅝ inch mark. This can be discarded. Now center the brown mat over the black mat so that the black shows evenly all around. This is best done by placing the brown over the black with both extending over the edge of the work table. When they are in proper alignment, tape the edge of the black to the **back** of the brown mat. Then turn the assembly over and finish taping around all four sides. When this is done, place the ⅜ inch wide strip that you saved inside the window of the brown mat and center the ⅜ strip so it makes an even black fillet (or even ¼ inch black pannel showing through at the outside edge of the strip) all around. Holding this in place, glue **gently and without excess glue,** one side of the strip. Hold this down on the brown until it is set. Glue the remaining three sides. The finished product is a split mat, ready for mounting the picture.

This is one of the few times gluing is recommended. Usually, neater work is done by taping mat elements together, but in this case the need for permanent support of the otherwise free-floating brown stripping makes glue preferable.

It is not often that the nonprofessional framer will be covering his own mats, but it's good to know the technique if the need arises. Two ways are often used, largely depending on whether the mat or board to be covered is the standard ⅛ inch matboard or a heavy craftboard ¼ inch or thicker.

The adhesive used in either case should make a good bond, be nonstaining, and be easy to handle. The easiest is probably the permanent spray adhesives which come commercially in spray cans. The other recommended adhesive is the 'white glue' so commonly in use and recommended earlier as the best general glue for the framer. If it is too thick, white glue can be thinned with water to a consistency easy to handle.

The covering material may be grasscloth, burlap, linen, velvet or velveteen, or even colored paper. Sometimes it is desirable to use a matching type of wallpaper in framing a picture, sometimes a piece of fabric found in the room for draperies, and so forth. This latter is less the case in fine art framing than in purely decorative work, but the procedure is exactly the same in either case.

Covering the thin matboard is the simpler procedure of the two. The mat should be cut to fit the rabbet measurement as always. A piece of the covering material, slightly larger than the mat, is then prepared. The mat is covered with adhesive—easier and simpler to control with the spray type as there is less problem of soaking the mat and causing subsequent cockling—and the material is laid on it face up. Then, with a soft rubber brayer (such as used in photography for rolling prints onto the ferrotype tins or the type used in block printing), the material is pressed with a rolling motion onto the matboard, rolling from the center toward the outside to eliminate any air bubbles. This should be done several times, particularly just before the glue sets, if the white plastic type glue is used. It is then wise to place weighted plywood or some other rigid surface over the covered mat until it is thoroughly dry.

Once the covered mat is dry, the outer edge should be carefully trimmed and the window marked for cutting. When cutting fabric, it is preferable to cut from the face; this will give a cleaner cut with less danger of raveling the threads and will not tend to pull the fabric loose from the mat, as might happen if the back-cutting technique is used.

For marking fabric, pencil is not advisable even if it is visible, because the marks are exceedingly difficult to remove. A pastel pencil or sharpened pastel stock is good as is an edged bit of tailor's chalk, the kind used for marking suits and other clothing for alterations. After the cut is made, these marks may be easily brushed off without damage to the fabric covering.

In covering the thicker mats, and these are generally beveled at the lip, it is customary to cover the lip as well. This means that the mat must be completely cut before the material is applied. When the mat is cut to proper dimensions, it is laid face down on the **back** of the material to be cut and the material is marked for cutting.

As diagram A below shows, the material should be about 1 inch wider both inside and outside than the mat it will cover.

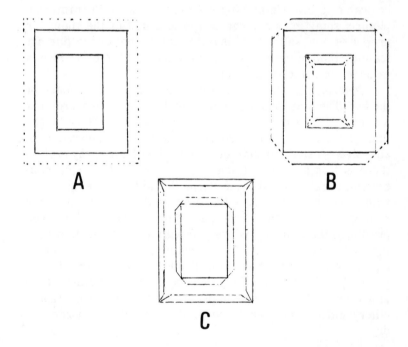

A

B

C

Mark the cloth and cut the outside and the opening. A very sharp knife (or scissors) is required. Lay the mat again on the cloth and cut out the corners inside and out as shown in B. Put glue on the mat, lay the fabric on and roll it firmly on the flat surface until it holds. Then carefully tuck the inner edges under the beveled lip and press the cloth down all around. Make sure there are no wrinkles or bubbles. Place the mat on the table, face of the cloth side **down,** and bring the back edges up and over the mat and glue them down also. A slight pulling pressure when bringing the edges around to the back for gluing will help keep the material smooth and tight. The black of the finished mat will look like diagram C. Place a weighted surface on this mat until it has dried completely.

No doubt you will find variations on styling and techniques with your own experimentation, but the foregoing will provide a firm basis for this as well as provide you with all you need for doing a professional job of matting.

SECTION C—ASSEMBLING

Tools for Frame Assembling

Tools required in the assembly of the completed framing job are few and most of them have already been mentioned. Some extra materials will be needed, however, including brown paper since all work under glass should be protected in the back by a brown paper dust cover.

A good glass cleaner and lintless cloth are essential. There are special glass cleaner formulas used by some framers for one reason or another, but on the whole, a commercially available spray cleaner is perfectly adequate for the job. It also has the advantage of being readily available around the home.

Brads of varying sizes for fastening in the glass and framed components are necessary unless you use the glazier's gun with points. The latter is a handy item, but the force of its spring can break open the corner of a fragile moulding or, if not handled with skill, can break the glass. On hardwoods and large frames, however, it is a boon.

If brads are used, they can be put in a hand tool known as the 'nail driver' which can be adjusted to set the nail at any depth and thus insure that it will not be pushed through the moudling, a frequent occurence with thin mouldings. For the nonprofessional, a pair of square-nose pliers (those used in glass cutting) will work very well if handled carefully.

A tack hammer is needed for those mouldings and jobs where strips must be nailed in or where nails are preferred for fastening in the assembled components. This is particularly true of Masonite drymounts or in cases where a back brace must be applied.

Nail sets, small drill and bits, and screw drivers, are all items which you will have had from earlier phases of framing as well as screws and brads. The sandpaper and block for finishing the backing and the white glue for putting on the dust cover were also previously mentioned.

The other additional materials will be brown paper for the dust cover, hardware for the finishing, including screw eyes, wire, sawtooth hangers, string, and if colored strips are used to mount a deep watercolor, some appropriate stains or paints.

For attaching oils to frames there is also need for flat strips of metal from time to time. As was discussed in the section on making frames, various corner braces may be needed.

Assembling Oils

As oils are comparatively simple to assemble and present fewer problems for the framer, it is better to begin with a discussion of how to assemble them. Oils are generally already on the stretcher bar when presented for framing. If not, this mounting onto the stretcher must be done before measurements can be made for the frame.

Framing of oils can be either simple or compound depending on whether one frame or several are used. In addition, there will be the problem with some oils where the stretcher bar will extend beyond the moulding and some where the moulding rabbet is deeper than the stretcher bar. In a few cases, the stretcher bar and the rabbeting of the moulding will be the same thickness. It will require a different technique for each. The same will apply to assembling several components in the frame itself, such as linen liners within cappings and so forth.

Let us remind you that if the stretcher bar is higher than the rabbeting so that it protrudes beyond the back of the frame, stripping is usually applied to make the appearance neater. This is shown in diagram A below. If the frame is compound, however, and the stretcher extends beyond the back of the linen liner **but not beyond the back of the frame as**

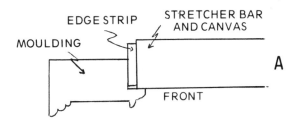

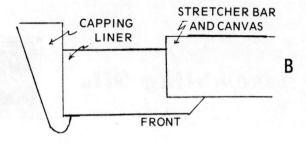

CAPPING LINER

STRETCHER BAR AND CANVAS

B

FRONT

a whole, such stripping is not required and merely adds extra work. See diagram B above.

The customary way for attaching one element to another has traditionally been by means of long nails set at an angle through the inner component into the surrounding one as shown below. First the hole is bored in the inner element to set the angle and to prevent splitting. The nail is driven, in **but not**

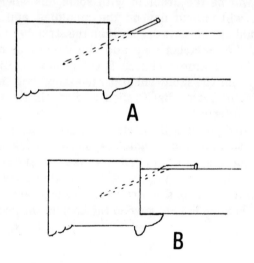

A

B

all the way (A). The tip of the nail is left extending a bit above the inner element and is then bent over (B). This not only prevents the inner element from being able to slip away from the front or outer element, it also makes it easier to remove the nail if for any reason the outer moulding has to be removed. The same system is used when nailing the stretcher and canvas to the surrounding frame element, and for the same reasons.

This technique has its drawbacks, however, chiefly because such nailing does not hold the elements firmly in place, especially since no fit is perfect. This is particularly noticeable in the case of large paintings and relatively thin mouldings. There is too much give or play when the work is handled by the frame. Small works with thin moulding or those with heavy frames have no such problem. In addition to this problem, current mouldings are seldom without some curvature. By utilizing the method indicated below, you will be able to use the stretcher bar and each succeeding element as a support for the adjoining one. The two following cases are exaggerated. In A, the nailing system is used and it is readily apparent that the curvature of the moulding cannot be corrected by the nail and will only become worse with time. In B, however, use of the screw eye and screw **pulls** the moulding inward to straighten and then hold it firmly. It is easier to remove than a nail and makes a far stronger frame than the nailing system.

If the stretcher bar and the frame rabbet are the same thickness, and if the surrounding element is a linen liner or some quality sturdy element, then nailing is perfectly all right and is much simpler than using strips or metal. If the surrounding element is a beading or some less sturdy

BACK VIEW

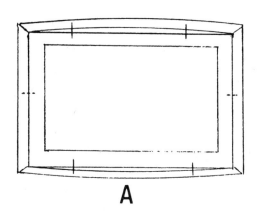

A

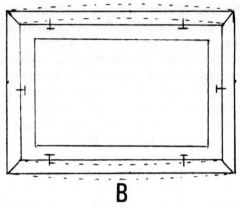

B

moulding, it will be better to fasten the stretcher bar to the moulding with strips of metal as shown below. These can be commercially available strips, inset if they are thick, or else thin strips of metal cut from a tin can or other sheeting and bored at either end. There is also the possibility of turnbuckles

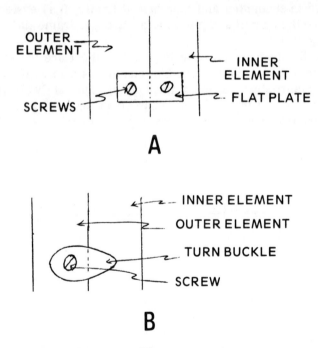

OUTER ELEMENT

INNER ELEMENT

FLAT PLATE

SCREWS

A

INNER ELEMENT

OUTER ELEMENT

TURN BUCKLE

SCREW

B

of the flat type as used in photographic work. These are very handy and will work well provided they are of sufficient size and strength. See diagram B above.

If the stretcher bar of the inner component is shallower than the rabbeting of the surrounding element, fastening is best done by putting screw eyes in the inner component as shown in diagram A below and then screwing this to the outer element. Diagram B shows the back of this assembly with

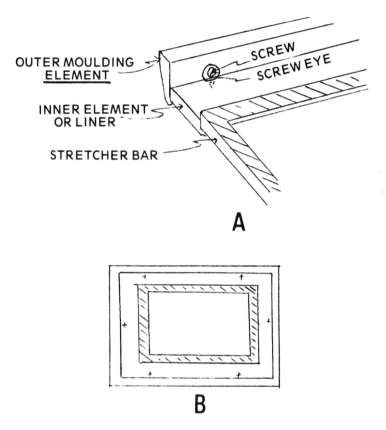

OUTER MOULDING ELEMENT

SCREW

SCREW EYE

INNER ELEMENT OR LINER

STRETCHER BAR

A

B

small crosses to indicate where the screw eyes should go. The larger the frame, naturally, the more screw eyes used. Also, if there is much curvature in the outer component, it is advisable to use more screw eyes, closer together, to correct this.

When the inner component is **higher** than the rabbeting of the outer element, the above system **will not work**. In this case, the screw eyes must be placed in the **outer** element as shown in the following illustration and the screws driven into the edge of the inner element. In all cases, screws of the appropriate size must be selected or they will split the moulding when driven in.

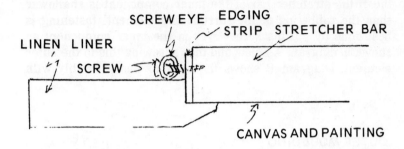

SCREW EYE EDGING STRIP STRETCHER BAR
LINEN LINER
SCREW
CANVAS AND PAINTING

Although some framers in the past have put dust covers on oil paintings, the most recent evidence indicates that this is more harmful than not in preserving the canvas from deterioration. A certain amount of aeration at the back of the canvas is necessary, so it is preferable to leave the back uncovered.

When assembling a drymounted or wetmounted work, since these are normally on Masonite or craftboard, no more than ¼ inch thick and usually closer to ⅛ inch, the work will be held in its surrounding frame element by brads or nails, the same as with other works to be discussed later. As mentioned earlier in the section on making the frame, large works are usually crossbraced in back.

If glazier's points are used for holding small oils, drymounts, or wetmounts into the frame, the effect is shown below. For nails, they are put in at a slight angle, driven deeper and then bent down to hold the work firmly. If nails are used and the wood of the frame is a hardwood, it is advisable to drill partially into the moulding first to ease the work.

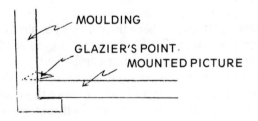

MOULDING
GLAZIER'S POINT
MOUNTED PICTURE

A typical cross section is shown on the following page where the stretcher bar is higher than the rabbet of the liner but lower than the rabbet of the outermost component, while the liner is also lower than the outside component.

The relative position of screw eyes is illustrated below in A. In the adjoining back view (B) of the assembly, small crosses show the position of screw eyes for attaching the stretcher bar

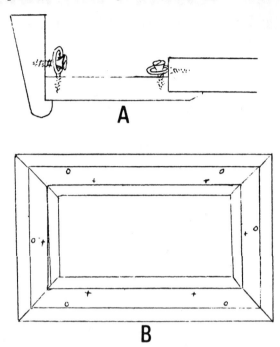

A

B

to the liner and small circles show those for attaching the liner to the capping.

The profile below shows how to handle the assembly when the stretcher bar is higher than the liner and the liner is in turn higher than the outer frame. Placement of the screw eyes

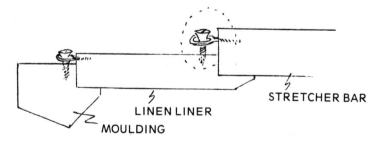

STRETCHER BAR

LINEN LINER

MOULDING

depends on clearance. The screw eyes (in the dotted circle above) could be mounted on the liner if the clearance is sufficient rather than in the stretcher bar, with the screws going into the bar instead of into the liner.

Assembling Works Under Glass

One of the most annoying difficulties in framing under glass is the problem of cleaning. Even after the most careful work, there always seems to be a mark on the inside of the glass and a piece of lint or dust on the surface of the mat. These must be removed, no matter how annoying or tedious the task may be, if the finished product is to look its best.

There is no need to go into detail about cleaning the glass as practically everyone has had some experience with it. Suffice to say that the glass must be absolutely clean on the inner surface as this cannot be reached once the work is assembled. Many framers clean only the inner surface, leaving the outer until after the finished assembly. Others prefer to clean both surfaces before assembly as this helps to reveal any fingermarks or other marks or streaks on the inner surface. It is helpful to tilt the glass from side to side and view it from an angle as many streaks cannot otherwise be seen.

Before laying the glass in the rabbet of the frame, check the rabbeting for dirt or unwanted particles and brush thoroughly with a stiff-bristled brush to dislodge any foreign bits. Check the corners to see that there are no protruding nail points or dried blobs of glue which would interfere with assembly and tend to break the glass when pressure is put on during the placing of brads or glazier's points.

When this is done, wipe the matted work carefully (an unfixed pastel should never be wiped, obviously, but the mat around it should) or brush it off to remove all foreign particles. **Clean all surfaces**, front, back, and even the edges. It is surprising how many small bits can cling to the edges, and the bits will be dislodged during the assembly.

Place the glass in the rabbet of the frame, which is laid face down on the assembly table, then place the matted work face down on that, and then put on the backing cardboard. This backing is a sheet of corrugated cardboard used to provide a firm support to prevent the work and the mat from buckling. Holding all in place with the fingers, lift the frame and all so that a last-minute check can be made to see that there are no unwanted marks on the glass or specks on the mat. When all is cleaned to satisfaction, put the work down and tack in the back. This, as discussed in the last chapter, may be done with either brads or glazier's points.

For driving in the diamond-shaped glazier's points, the special gun is needed. If brads are being used, however, they may be put in with either the nail driver or pushed in with the pliers. (The nail driver, previously mentioned, is very good for the purpose but is not worth the investment for any but the professional framer.) A pair of wide-jaw pliers may be used if the jaw which will go against the moulding is covered with plastic foam, soft leather, or similar covering, to prevent the jaw from marring the moulding. For this, lay the nail down on the backing with the point toward the moulding, and then settle the jaws of the pliers over it and the moulding, so that by squeezing the jaws together, you force the nail into the moulding. Care is needed as it is very hard to judge the pressure; in the softer woods, the nail may easily come through the other side and be clinched or bent over before the action can be arrested.

One of the easiest systems to use, provided a bit of care is exercised, is to use the flat side of the square-nose pliers to force the nail in. This is shown below. Keep your thumb on the

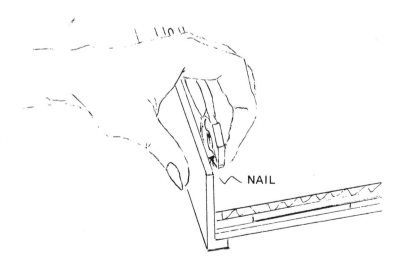

NAIL

outside of the moulding and provide the support for squeezing the pliers against the head of the nail. CAUTION—Your thumb should **not** be held in the spot where the point of the nail will come through if too much pressure is applied or it will be driven into your thumb! Many woods such as pine have very hard grain striations with soft wood in between. The nail could be blocked at such a hard striation, forcing you to exert more than usual pressure to force the nail further. When the nail suddenly passes through the tough part of the wood it will practically shoot through the remaining moulding. For this reason, keep your thumb quite clear of the possible danger. With a bit of experience, you will have no difficulty in judging this change of pressure.

In some instances, generally with pastels, photographs, and delicate work of the nature of paintings on leaves or mounted fragile things, it is desirable to prevent the work from coming into contact with the glass when a mat is not being used. If the clearance required to prevent contact is very little, a length of cord or a thin strip of matting, sometimes called a **ghost**, may be glued along the glass where it will be hidden by the rabbet as shown below. The mat strip is usually more successful than the cord but a bit more difficult

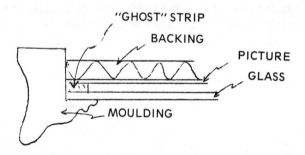

to cut. Take care that the width of the material is less than the lip of the rabbet or it will be visible from the front.

In other cases, a more exaggerated form of the same problem occurs. This may be handled by the use of the shadow box moulding, a typical instance of which is shown next in A, which is very convenient with its double rabbeting. If a regular moulding such as a capping is used for the frame, but this same shadow-box effect is wanted, then inner wood strips

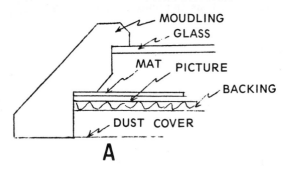

FACE OR FRONT

MOUDLING
GLASS
MAT PICTURE
BACKING
DUST COVER

A

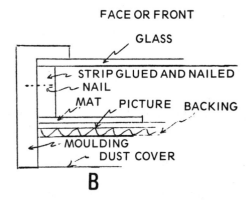

FACE OR FRONT

GLASS
STRIP GLUED AND NAILED
NAIL
MAT PICTURE BACKING
MOULDING
DUST COVER

B

must be inserted after the glass and nailed or glued to hold them in place. This is shown above in diagram B. It is customary to wait until after this inner stripping is down before cleaning the glass.

The dimensions of the strips will vary with each frame and set of conditions, so it is impossible to give any exact measurements. Several things are common to all such projects, however. First, the stripping must not be so thick that it is wider than the lip of the rabbet—but it must be thick enough to hold the matted work. Second, the stripping must give the proper separation between the glass and the work, but it must be shallow enough so that it allows the matted work and the backing to go into the frame and be tacked in properly. These strips may be mitered for a perfect fit inside or they may be just long enough to come to the corners and touch without a miter. Such a corner is shown below. It does not matter which method is used, as the whole system is sealed, but the latter is easier.

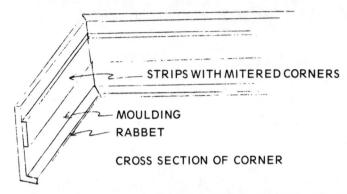

STRIPS WITH MITERED CORNERS

MOULDING
RABBET

CROSS SECTION OF CORNER

This stripping is usually painted black or stained a deep color to make it as unobtrusive as possible, as must be the inner side of the first rabbeting when the double-rabbeted shadow box is used. There may be cases, though, where a different color will do more to enhance the work. The ultimate choice is again a matter for the framer or for the person having the framing done.

It is also possible to create a "depth" effect by putting the mat against the glass at the front of the frame, and the work, also matted if desired, against the back strip or second rabbet. If this is done, painting the inner stripping is less important, but again it must be cautioned that the strips (if used) must be put in after the glass and first mat. Also in this case, the glass

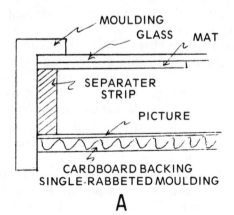

MOULDING
GLASS   MAT

SEPARATER
STRIP

PICTURE

CARDBOARD BACKING
SINGLE-RABBETED MOULDING

A

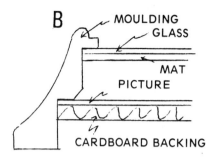

B

MOULDING
GLASS
MAT
PICTURE

CARDBOARD BACKING

DOUBLE-RABBETED MOULDING

should be cleaned before the mat is placed against it. This assembly is shown on the bottom of the previous page and above in cross section.

After the assembly of glass and other components and after the tacking in of the assembled works, it is necessary to put on a dust cover (**not recommended for oils**). This will keep out extraneous grit and atmospheric pollution to a great extent and will protect the work against humidity changes to a substantial degree. The dust cover is really a sheet of brown

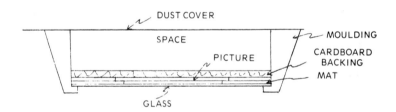

DUST COVER
SPACE
PICTURE
MOULDING
CARDBOARD BACKING
MAT
GLASS

wrapping paper, a heavier type being required on larger framing, which is glued to the back edge or base of the moulding. The diagram above shows its position.

To make this cover, cut a piece of brown paper larger than the frame dimensions by several inches. Dampen it slightly and lay it aside. Now take the white glue, which should be in a squeeze bottle with spout, and squeeze a steady thread of this glue along the back of the moulding as shown in diagram A. Rub this out with the finger so that it spreads and coats the back edge thoroughly. With smaller, thinner mouldings, the glue should cover the whole back of the moulding.

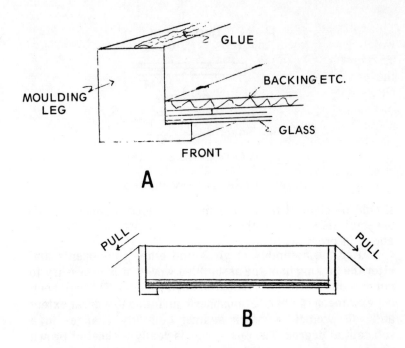

GLUE

BACKING ETC.

MOULDING
LEG

GLASS

FRONT

A

PULL

PULL

B

Place the paper over the back and carefully pull it outward and downward over the edges of the moulding all around, as in diagram B above. Hold it in place on one side while stretching it on the other or it will slide off the first side. Now rub it down with the hands all around a few times. Within a couple of minutes, the glue will begin to set.

When the glue has set, wait a few minutes longer and then, with sandpaper on a sanding block, run the sandpaper along the back edge at a 45 deg angle as shown in the diagram below.

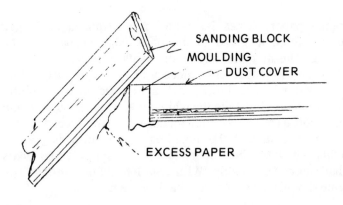

SANDING BLOCK
MOULDING
DUST COVER

EXCESS PAPER

This will sand off the excess paper neatly and leave a clean job which no amount of trimming any other way could produce. There may be wrinkles along the edges from the expansion of the paper while wet with glue, just as there will be some ripples in the backing paper itself from being dampened. Have no concern. When the paper dries, all these will stretch out to give a flat paper which is tight as a drumhead. This tightness provides additional support to the whole frame.

If a liner is used inside a capping, the dust cover should come to the edges of the liner or inner element rather than over the whole capping. This should be put on before the inner element is inserted and fastened into the outer capping.

At times, artists who exhibit their work prefer the work within the frame not to be permanent and a system is used to allow rapid changing of the frame contents. In this case, no backing is applied as it would have to be removed each time, providing more of a hindrance than a help. Don't use glazier's points to hold in the contents, as they are not always easy to remove, and after a time, will chew up the frame moulding. Use brads, making sure they are returned to the same holes as often as possible and pushing them in only far enough to hold the contents firm.

Very best of all in this situation are turnbuckles. These should be of the flat type shown below which will not project in

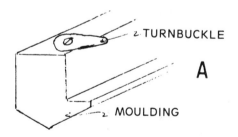

the back to hold the frame out from the wall, and they should be mounted at the rim of the moulding as in diagram A above. In those cases where the backing is below the level of the moulding edge, either additional layers of corrugated cardboard may be put in over the backing or small blocks, as in diagram B, may be used to provide the tension.

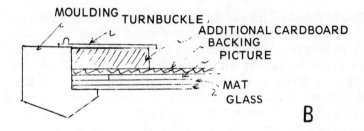

In some instances, where the rabbeting is very shallow and a triple mat is used, the level of the backing will be above the moulding surface, as shown in the diagram below. Since glazier's points cannot be used, nails should be put through the cardboard and at a distance far enough back (as shown) so

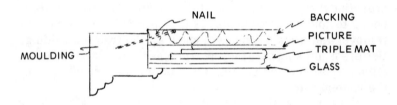

that the heads will not protrude. This will allow the backing to be put on as before. If turnbuckles are to be used, raiser blocks (as shown below) will provide the clearance for the turnbuckles.

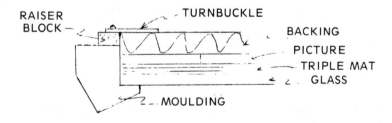

After the backing is put on, some arrangement is necessary for hanging the framed picture. The system in most common usage is screw eyes and wire. A screw eye should be put into the thickest part of the moulding between one-quarter and one-third of the length down from the top on either side. Then a wire of sufficient strength to hold the weight, with a safety factor to insure that the wire will not break, should be strung from one side to the other, allowing enough slack so that the picture will hang flat against the wall. There is usually a bit of stretching of the wire after it is hung as all the small kinks and curves in the wire will pull straight due to the weight of the framed picture. The figure below shows the approximate position for the screw eyes and a detailed diagram of how the wire should be fastened around the screw eye.

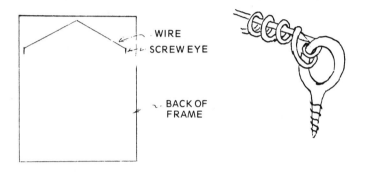

WIRE
SCREW EYE

BACK OF
FRAME

About 6 inches of extra wire should be left on each side to twist around after the wire has been led **twice** through the opening in the screw eye.

When thin mouldings such as cappings frame a heavy work, one screw eye per side is often not sufficient to hold the weight involved. It may be necessary to use two or even three screw eyes in a row as indicated in the diagram below. Thread the wire as shown and fasten it at both ends in the top and bottom screw eyes. All the wire strands must be over the support when the picture is hung.

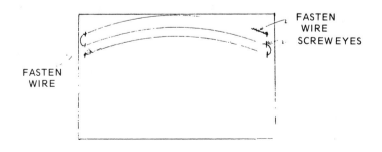

FASTEN
WIRE
SCREW EYES

FASTEN
WIRE

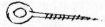

When buying screw eyes for framing, take care to get the short-shanked variety with a deep thread as shown at the left above. The long-shanked screw eyes are really not suitable for framing unless one has a very heavy moulding, and even then these tend to have rather shallow threads which may pull out of the moulding after a time. In addition, they hold the picture too far from the wall unless they can be put all the way in so that only the eye protrudes, a difficult thing with flatter type mouldings. They also produce a lever effect, tending to pull them loose. The diagram below shows the proper position of the short-shanked screw eye in contrast to the improper positioning of one which is too long.

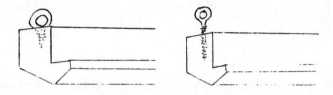

On heavy frames it may be safer and desirable to use the swivel or ring-type eye with a support plate which can be put into the moulding with several screws. One such example is shown in diagrams A and B. These are very effective and worth the additional cost.

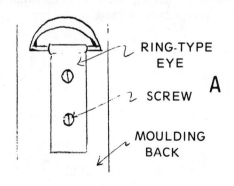

RING-TYPE EYE

SCREW **A**

MOULDING BACK

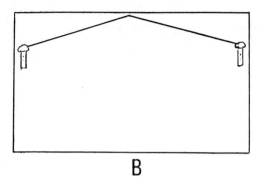

B

Yet another type of hanger is the sawtooth variety shown below. This is centered on the top length of moulding and fastened by special brads at each end. They hold the picture to the wall quite flat and can be adjusted to make the picture level by hanging to a tooth right or left of the center. These are really for smaller, relatively lightweight pictures and care should be exercised in trying to use them for larger work.

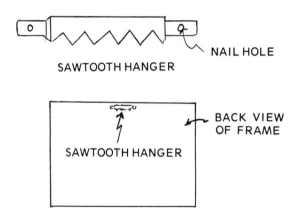

NAIL HOLE

SAWTOOTH HANGER

BACK VIEW
OF FRAME

SAWTOOTH HANGER

Some framers use little rubber feet or blocks at the lower corners of the frame to compensate for the screw eyes as shown on the next page. This is generally an unnecessary refinement but, as with other extras, is a matter of personal taste.

Occasionally there will be a demand for the "decorator cord" for hanging a picture. These are usually cloth-wound

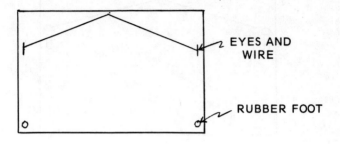

EYES AND WIRE

RUBBER FOOT

wires with rosettes or some other decorative item at the top to cover the nail or hook for hanging or else plain cords with the hook itself covered by a decorative facing. They are made to run above the picture and to be visible.

SECTION D—
MISCELLANEOUS
TECHNIQUES

Finishes for Frames

Unless you are interested in spending a lot of time in the finishing of raw wood frames or the alteration of previously finished frames, you are better off to buy finished mouldings in the beginning. It is very rare indeed to find even a skillful framer who can rival the commercial finishes on frames, and the time spent is enormous compared to the results. Such processes as leafing can be done by the individual after considerable practice, though the results are still rarely equal to the professional level, but the variety of commercial finishes is obviously beyond the scope of the individual—especially the beginner.

It is only infrequently that you will want to concern yourself with intricate do-it-yourself finishes. While hand carving, leafing, simulated antiquing with multicolor speckling, crackle finish panels, and so forth, sound most intriguing in theory (and **are** very attractive), they are not easy to achieve in practice with any degree of consistency and are not recommended for the beginner.

However, there are some processes for finishing which can be applied by the beginner that will give very good results and which do not need a thousand dollars worth of extra equipment to make them practical. The simplest of these are common, commercial wood stains with a shellac sealer and a good wax finish.

There are a number of stains on the market. In general, they are either water-soluble or turpentine-soluble base types. Water-soluble stains are used by some mass manufacturers because of the lower toxicity factor in use of solvents and the ease of application. The chief disadvantage in water-soluble stains is that they raise the grain in the wood, that is, the soft part and the harder grain absorb water in unequal amounts, causing the grain in the wood to become more prominent. This usually returns to normal on drying, but sometimes it does not.

The two chief advantages of the turpentine-soluble or "oil-based" stains are that a large selection is available and that the staining does not affect the surface of the wood. Penetration into the wood also seems deeper in most comparable cases. Again, the choice is left to you. If stains are used containing naphtha and other solvents, as the **oil-based** are, they must be used in well ventilated areas. In any case, **when using stains or preparations of any kind the manufacturer's recommendations and cautions should be carefully followed.**

In finishing wood, the fundamental and exceedingly important step is preparing the wood. Various types of wood will react differently to staining. Hardwoods are generally easier to handle but take the stain less readily. You will learn this by experience. You will soon note, for example, that pine always looks streaky because the grain, which absorbs less stain, will be lighter than the softer wood in between. Basswood is often used in making mouldings, but it has a tendency to take stain unevenly, absorbing stain in spots which always appear darker than the surrounding areas. There are ways to avoid this, but they require experience. Hardwoods, such as bird's-eye maple and oak, take stain less easily, and if a dark color is desired, the stain must be concentrated before application.

It is often said that if the first application of a stain is not sufficient, further coats will darken the wood to the desired shade. This is true only within limits. Each coat of stain acts to some extent as a sealer, inhibiting the effect of subsequent coats. Therefore, although a very dark stain can be achieved with the first coat by using the concentrated stain, several coats of a diluted and lighter stain will almost never reach the same saturation. Hardwoods in general will not stain so darkly as porous or soft woods.

Before the stain is applied, sand the wood with a very fine sandpaper, No. 00 or No. 000. Some framers give the raw wood a rubbing down with steel wool in addition. This initial smoothing of the wood will determine how good a finish can ultimately be put on it. No finish can possibly be better than the preparation for its application.

Stains may be applied either as they are or thinned down with the appropriate solvent. Most framers will want to dilute the stains for lighter finishing. The manufacturer's directions give detailed instructions. As a general rule, you will learn what suits you best by trial and error.

Uniform stains are a bit difficult to achieve. One of the greatest and most common mistakes is to try staining a small bit at a time. This inevitably leads to a splotchy result which cannot be corrected without a lot of difficult sanding and often not even then. The method described below seems to give the best results for hand staining.

First prepare as much stain as will be needed for the frame. Do this by mixing enough of the well stirred staining solution with the proper amount of additional solvent (we shall assume turpentine-and oil-based stains for our discussion) to give the depth of stain required in sufficient quantity. Mix up only the required amount for each job or waste will result.

We save the miter cuts from their mouldings so that stain mixtures may be tried on them for suitability before applying to the face of the frame. If you have not saved miter cuts or have run out of them (and you must try the stain on the same piece of wood you are going to stain), then turn the frame over and try the stain on the back or base of the moulding where it will never show.

When the frame has been sanded and thoroughly wiped off with a lintless cloth to remove all dust and foreign particles, dip a pad of flannel or other cloth in the stain mixture and apply it with a smooth, continuous sweep of the arm the full length of the moulding side from miter corner to miter corner. It is best to do the first wipe across the back of the leg since this edge, being perpendicular to the wall, will be less obvious if there is any mistake. Then wipe the stain along the other surfaces of the same side. If the wipe is smooth and continuous from one corner to another, there will be no irregular splotches and edges showing.

Although the pad of cloth is standard and recommended by the manufacturers almost universally, it seldom holds enough stain to really cover some of the larger surfaces in one wipe across. For this reason, we suggest that you try cutting off the end of one of the fine-textured plastic sponges and using it. Be careful; sponge will absorb a very great amount of stain which will spurt in all directions if you're not alert. With care, however, the sponge covers the larger surfaces beautifully and will hold sufficient stain to work easily into the cracks and corners—something difficult to accomplish with the cloth pad.

When such a piece of sponge has been used—for one or for several frames if they are all to receive the same stain—it must be discarded as it will deteriorate very soon after use.

Such a sponge will harden if left overnight, for example, to dry. If any attempt is made to use it further, it will begin to crumble and prove useless. There is no economy in trying to be sparing with such bits of sponge.

After the stain has been applied over the whole frame, it should be left to dry. Again follow the manufacturer's instructions. Overnight is normally a good and sufficient time. After the stain is thoroughly dry, it must be sealed into the wood so application of finishing wax, speckling or other operations will not affect it. This is done by applying shellac.

Shellac is obtainable in white or clear and in orange tones. The orange shellac imparts a slightly warmer tone to the work. For the nonprofessional, the clear or white is recommended. Shellac should be purchased in the smallest needed amounts, as it does not keep indefinitely. There are several grades available of which the most common are the "4-pound" and "8-pound cut." This means that either four or eight pounds of the basic resin have been dissolved in a gallon of solvent. The 4-pound cut is better for sealing the stain, and in some cases it is desirable to make it a bit thinner by addition of more shellac thinner or denatured alcohol. The 8-pound cut, if available, can be converted to 4-pound cut by diluting it in a ratio of one part shellac mixture to one part thinner.

The shellac may be applied by brush or by pad. A pad of soft cloth is very good and permits you to rub the shellac into corners and crevices without getting tears or gobs building up. This shellac coat must be left to dry thoroughly. After it is dry, sand the shellac coat down or work it down with steel wool or a plastic pad (such as the Scotch-Brite) until it is very smooth and even. Then wipe it off by rubbing with a soft cloth. The finishing wax may then be applied, but it is preferable to put on a second coat of shellac. This not only insures the sealing of the stain but provides a much smoother finish to the final appearance. The second coat is applied the same as the first and, when dry, again rubbed down and wiped off.

If a shiny varnish coat is desired, this can be put on with a good quality varnish according to the manufacturer's instructions. The current trend, however, favors the softer, silkier effect of waxing.

The two basic waxes for frame finishing are carnauba wax and beeswax. Carnauba wax is harder and will give more shine and a somewhat tougher protective coat, but beeswax is probably more common. A standard mixture for the beeswax is one part beeswax to three parts turpentine, and many professional framers add a small amount of microcrystalline wax as a plasticizer. The easiest system for making it is to melt the beeswax and microcrystalline wax together in a can sitting in a pan of boiling water, and then removing it far from the heat for safety (turpentine is volatile and flammable). Stir in the turpentine slowly to make the paste. If this mixture hardens in cool weather, it may be warmed slightly before use.

Application of the wax is best done with the fingers. Rub it in well and leave it for a few minutes. Then, using steel wool or the plastic pad, gently go over the whole frame to remove excess wax. When this has been done, rub briskly with lamb's wool or a soft cloth to impart sheen and finish.

There are preparations on the market in which the stain is prepared with a wax in the solvent so that the sealing with shellac and the final waxing are not necessary. These are perfectly adequate for the nonprofessional and much easier to use, but they almost always require an additional waxing or oil-finishing to really protect them. In most cases the manufacturers market an additional "oil finish" or "wax finish" to be used as a final step.

The usual household waxes and automobile waxes, particularly the liquid forms, are **not recommended** for use in framing.

In addition to the above, you will find a number of stain-varnish preparations available. These, because of their varnish base, are more difficult for proper application and are somewhat limited in value for use in framing. They are **not** recommended for the nonprofessional framer.

Another useful type finish is that which is sold under various trade names in "antiquing kits." These offer a variety of finishes and are relatively easy to apply. Since they are specifically marketed for amateur use in wood finishing, they are quite foolproof if directions are followed, and the results are fully acceptable. The only caution is that they work better on some surfaces than on others. Raw woods, particularly oak, take these finishes surprisingly well. Other woods, particularly bass and virola or others with no appreciable grain, take the base coat very well but provide no adequate grain for holding the "glaze" which is rubbed on after the base coat dries. When using such antiquing preparations, it is preferable not to sand too greatly. A roughened surface is necessary for the proper effect.

There are a number of paints and enamels available in spray cans which will serve well. They are more expensive than bulk paints, but their convenience makes them particularly well suited to the occasional framer who is not doing production work. Directions are listed on the can.

Some but not all of the plastic-based paints are also suited for finishing frames. Latex-based paints that are currently available tend to be vulnerable to finger marks and other soiling and do not clean easily or well. The acrylic polymers and similar products are preferable and can be cleaned with water without damage to the finish if the cleaning is done carefully. Most of these look better if they are not waxed after drying.

Occasionally you will want to darken a color to age it or even put a coating over gold leaf to make it appear aged. This may be done by mixing a little burnt umber with turpentine and sometimes a bit of linseed oil and then mixing it into the needed quantity of varnish to obtain a slight coloring. This will make a suitable darkening glaze. Needless to say, other colors, especially aniline dyes, may also be used in this manner.

Casein paints have always been popular for finishing frames as they are water-soluble and dry to a waterproof covering. They may be put on quite heavily to obtain impasto results which may be combed through or otherwise textured, and they are quick-drying. It is not always easy to find them for sale in large enough quantity for the framer as they appear to be less popular than the new plastic-based products. They seem to be superseded in large part by these new paints and, at least from a practical standpoint, have no appreciable advantage over the plastics except that they are more brittle when dry and hold peaks and edges more sharply. Contemporary plastic paints tend to flow more and to round off edges and peaks. In some cases, this is not desirable.

There is little reason to enter into involved discussion of leafing frames as the leafed frame is not of much interest to the nonprofessional or even to the professional except in special cases. As for gilding or bronzing a frame, there are many products on the market which may be used for this. None of them in our experience come close to duplicating gold leaf, but they are serviceable for providing a gold-like effect. In general, these preparations are not gold but bronze or other alloys and will tarnish if left exposed to air. For this reason, when they are used, they should be lacquered over or sprayed with one of the many clear plastic sprays to protect them from oxidizing.

To give variation and interest to otherwise single-colored frames, you might consider spattering the undercoat (once it is dry) with one or more other colors. For example, a medium gray base coat can be livened and made to look rich and sparkling by the spattering of black and red dots with just a bit of "gold." The simplest tool for this spattering is the toothbrush. Add one color at a time by spattering it on and allowing it to dry before the next color is added. To spatter, merely dip the end bristles lightly in the desired color (which should be of a moderately heavy consistency) and then, using either your thumb tip or a piece of wood or screen wire, rub along the bristles from front to back so that the paint will be spattered on the frame, which is placed face up on a flat surface such as the floor. Newspapers or a similar protecting sheet should be spread underneath the frame and for a distance around it—the paint will spatter in all directions! The size of the dots may be varied by changing the consistency of the paint mixture and by the amount on the brush as well as by the method of rubbing the bristles. Only experimentation can inform you on the detailed points.

"Panels," the broad strips of color running along the center of a moulding, can be added quite easily by the use of a small sash brush. This is a beveled brush, shown below, used

SASH BRUSH

for touching up or painting narrow surfaces along an edge. By holding the brush so that the tip is against one edge of the

panel for the first stroke and then reversing it for the next, a neat job can be accomplished. The previous diagram shows a typical moulding profile with the brush in place for painting one side of the panel. The panel might be a dark green over a black color or a black panel on gold or green. The base color should be applied overall first and allowed to dry before the "paneling" is attempted.

Quite accurate small lines may be added to a moulding by resting a straightedge along the frame top, loading a small, round brush (such as a watercolor brush) with paint and then, resting the hand on the straightedge and keeping the brush ferrule against the edge for guidance, drawing the line smoothly with equal pressure along the moulding. Enough paint should be loaded so that the line can be made in one stroke. This is illustrated below. It is seldom that more than

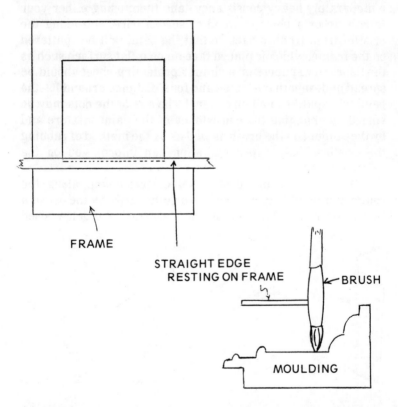

FRAME

STRAIGHT EDGE
RESTING ON FRAME

BRUSH

MOULDING

one line should be attempted on a frame as it is easy to overdo, and a "busy" or fussy effect results.

A good type of "driftwood" effect for large seascapes can be produced on a moulding of the type shown below by painting it overall first with a heavy coat of flat white paint, either plastic-based or casein, and then overpainting (when thoroughly dried) with a neutral gray made by mixing some

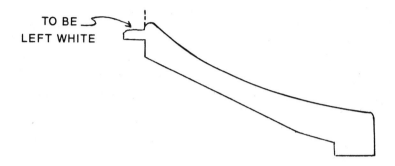

TO BE
LEFT WHITE

raw umber with the white. The lip of the moulding should be left white to add a sparkle or light effect to the moulding, as indicated. Before the gray has thoroughly dried but after it has set, a wire brush run along the surface will cut through the gray coating to expose the white undercoat in thin scratches. Allow this to dry thoroughly and then spatter the gray portion with fine black specks.

To prevent the spattering from falling on the white lip, use a cardboard shield as shown below to protect it. The spattering

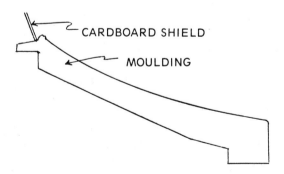

CARDBOARD SHIELD

MOULDING

is best done with a toothbrush and thumb as the other hand will be needed to hold the shield in place and to move it along the moulding as the spattering is done.

Limning or pickling can be done on wood by staining first or by leaving the wood in its natural state and rubbing white or some other color into the grain. Oak is one of the best woods for this treatment although chestnut and other woods respond well. It is necessary to have some grain prominent, however, or there will be no "grooves" to catch the white and hold it.

The recommended system for achieving this effect is to dip a pad of cloth such as folded cheesecloth into the white paint—or whatever color is being used—and then to rub this with a circular motion all over the area to be limned. After the surface has been covered so that all the grain has picked up some white, take another good-sized pad of the material and rub with pressure across the grain only. Press hard enough to wipe all the superfluous white off the smooth and raised parts of the wood but do not press the pad down into the grain striations nor wipe with the grain. If this is done, the color will be wiped away from wanted areas and the effect will be largely lost.

This same effect may be accomplished in soft, rather grainless woods by first scoring them lightly with coarse sandpaper (No. 2 is usually sufficient) or by brushing them with a wire brush of the type housepainters use to brush off old paint flakes before repainting. Another excellent tool for brushing finishes or for lightly scoring soft wood is the type of circular wire brush sold for use with the ¼ inch power drill. Being round, the wire brush circle fits the hand well and the bristles, close together and moderately stiff, seem to be just the right stiffness for texturing and combing. The rounded shape also allows maximum control. A pad of cloth over the top will protect the hand while the brush is being used or a glove may be worn if this proves a problem, but if the brush is held firmly with the fingers gripped over the center wheel, padding or gloves should not be necessary. It should be noted that such a brush should be used sideways to its normal position when used in hand combing.

Occasionally it will be desired to deeply score or mar a moulding to provide a special finish. This is known as "distressing" and may be accomplished with almost any instrument at hand. An icepick is fine, multiple icepicks even better. Scraps of glass, or bits of scrap iron, are used, as are the stiffer wire-bristled brushes. For those occasions where a really deep distressing is desirable, the ¼ inch electric drill with the brush attachment will gouge out a fine, rough surface in quick time. Softer woods with touch graining such as chestnut may be treated in this manner to produce beautiful effects.

After distressing on grainy woods, it is possible to achieve rich effects by using two or more layers of paint treated so the bottom layers show through the top. This is basically the method we described earlier for the "seascape" framing and is the basis underlying the "Venetian" effect in gilding where the red of the gilder's bole shows through the gold leaf. Artists will recognize it as the same principle as "graffitti" art. To produce such an effect, select three colors (more difficult to handle properly and two giving not enough contrast except in some few cases mentioned before) and paint them on the frame one over the other, being certain that each coat is allowed to dry thoroughly before applying the next coat. Assume that for the example we select a first coat of white, the second green, and the top or outer coat, gray. After the successive layers are dry, with either steel wool or fine sandpaper, go over the work lightly until the colors below begin showing through the covering coat or coats.

If the wood is grained or textured, the ridged parts will soon be sanded through to the white undercoat and even, if desired, down to the bare wood. This gives a weathered, old look to the wood which is prevented from being dull by the bits of white showing through. In other places, the sanding should not go beyond the green layer or the white layer. If the paint layers are rather thick, it might be preferable to sand down with a coarser paper first and then finish with a fine-grade paper. When the frame is sanded to satisfaction, it may be spattered with black and red, even a bit of yellow, before being shellacked and waxed or varnished. Or the frame may be left as it is without further protection, although it is best to finish the paint with something, if only a coat or two of shellac.

For the More Adventuresome

14

Strangely enough, framing has shown little inclination toward drastic changes over the decades. Moulding styles change, decorator approaches change, but the concept of framing seems securely locked in the idea of the rectangle holding work on all sides (plus the oval and the fan-shaped frames, of course). There has been little effort to produce open framing or different framing styles. The advanced framer or beginner might find some of our modifications on existing styles interesting, if only as a point of departure. But before going on to these, let us look at some of the techniques which are more generally found.

One of the more common styles of framing currently is that of mounting the painting or other work onto a wide, flat background. The two major styles for this involve either the floating type (different from the floating moulding) or the flat type. In the floating type, the work is framed as desired and then mounted against a finished background on invisible blocks which suspend it above or in front of the background surface. This is shown in diagrams A and B.

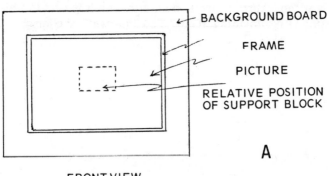

BACKGROUND BOARD

FRAME

PICTURE

RELATIVE POSITION OF SUPPORT BLOCK

A

FRONT VIEW

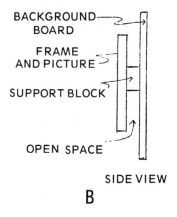

The background may be painted wood or other material or it may be fabric-covered, combed-finish paint, weathered boards, cork panels or practically any surface the framer can imagine. This is true, incidentally, of the covering for any of the **flats** used for background mounting as we shall discuss later.

In the other system of mounting, the moulding around the work is attached directly to the background, leaving no space between background and work. This is shown in illustrations C and D.

The first or floating style is less versatile than the flat or direct mount and looks somewhat too informal for many uses. It does give great dimension to the work, however, making it feel almost three-dimensional, and is often favored for abstracts or the more recent op-pop styles.

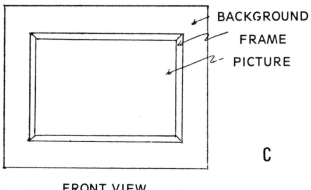

BACKGROUND
FRAME
PICTURE

C

FRONT VIEW

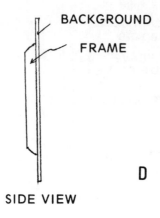

BACKGROUND

FRAME

D

SIDE VIEW

It should be noted that in either system of mounting to a background, the work should be framed first, at least with a simple capping, and then mounted. Before mounting, the background itself must be prepared and covered with whatever is to be used.

Framing of the work is exactly the same as discussed in the sections on framing and presents no new problems. It is only cautioned that the moulding used should not be too ornate. When using the flat mount, the moulding should not be so fragile that mounting it proves a problem. This is no problem with the floating type as the moulding is not important in the mounting. For the direct or flat type, however, screws will be used for mounting and the moulding should be thick enough to take the screws.

For small works, **tempered** Masonite may be used for the background base. For larger work, wood or composition board is preferable unless the Masonite is cradled, a bracing process which will be explained later. There are advantages and disadvantages to any material used. Masonite unless cradled will tend to curve, and the edges and corners are vulnerable to denting or crushing. Composition boards will crumble if the edges or corners are hit hard and are often difficult to cut properly without special equipment and, despite manufacturer's claims, many of them also warp. Wood, either plywood or pine boards, is often used for the background base. However, it is becoming more difficult every year to find plywood in the quarter-inch and half-inch thicknesses which are flat enough to be used in framing. It is amazing how warped and wavy the so-called "cured" laminated products can be. We have tried numerous materials, including the plastic foams and not been pleased with the results. Plywood, assuming that truly flat pieces can be obtained, is probably the best material.

Cork, metallic wallpapers, and plastic sheetings have all been used to provide coverings for the background, but paint and fabric are still the standards. If paint or thin papers are to be used, the edges of the background must be sanded very smooth and, if plywood, filled so that a neat edge is obtained. The covering material should be bent over the edge and around to the back because the edges will be visible on the finished work.

Painting requires no explanation. Materials such as paper which are pliable and easy to handle require little more. Put the adhesive (either a thinned white plastic glue or the spray-type adhesive) on the background and, if needed, on the back surface of the material, lay it on the background and roll it with the brayer until it is smoothly down. Then turn the edges over carefully, press them down to make them adhere smoothly, then turn the background over and glue the excess to the back.

Brittle material, such as cork sheets, requires previous alignment and then a gluing on sheet-by-sheet to obtain a neat job. Some cork sheets may be folded around the edge but most of them will break. It is best to trim the cork at the edges and then paint the edges of the background with a matching paint.

Fabrics, particularly the heavier fabrics such as decorator burlap and linen, require a bit more involved approach. Again, the face surface of the background should be coated with a proper adhesive, but far more liberally than for the paper or thin materials. (There are also special adhesives on the market for just this purpose if you feel impelled to buy them.) Wheat paste is the standard, traditional adhesive for professional framers. The new plastic adhesives do very well and are more resistant to humidity and mildew.

The fabric, as shown next, should be 3 or 4 inches larger in both dimensions than the measurement of the background. Lay the cloth on a flat surface, either floor or table, and then place the background board face (and adhesive) down on it. Bring one edge around and over the back where it will be glued into place. At this point, it is desirable to use a hand power

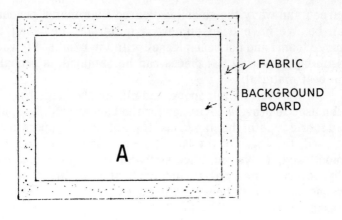

FABRIC

BACKGROUND
BOARD

A

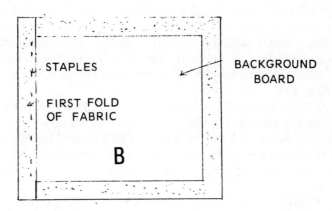

STAPLES

FIRST FOLD
OF FABRIC

B

BACKGROUND
BOARD

stapler to staple the edge down firmly as shown in diagram B
above. Now gently pull the other edge of the fabric around to
the back and repeat the gluing and stapling process. The whole
thing may now be lifted to see that the fabric is taut across the
face of the background and that the warp and woof of the
fabric are straight. Wavy lines caused by uneven stretching of
the fabric make an unsightly finished product. If the fabric is
wavy or at an angle to the edges of the background, one side
should be lifted and the correction made.

Next, one of the adjoining sides should be spread with glue
for folding over the fabric. If the fabric is merely folded over,
the lump caused by the excess cloth at the fold may prove
unwelcome. There are two ways of dealing with this. In the

figure below, A shows how the excess may be cut away so that the side may be folded over without adding an additional thickness to the corner while yet leaving enough to insure full coverage of the edge. In B, the fabric is merely folded down a bit further, slanting the edge downward or inward to prevent the corner from bulking up. The method of B avoids the risk of raveling, but since the fabric is glued and in very little danger of raveling, either method should work very well.

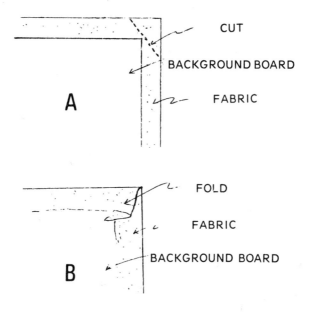

After this, you may proceed with whichever one of the two styles of mounting you wish. If the floating type is wanted (and this is easiest with painting on panels where the panel may be directly mounted to the block or blocks) a block, or four blocks close to the center, are mounted securely by drilling holes and putting screws in from the back. If the work is small and a panel, it is merely glued to the blocks, making sure that it is correctly centered. The amount of such background edging should never be less than 3 inches and is usually better if 4 or 5 inches, and as much as 8 to 10 inches for large works.

Paintings which are capped with deep-rabbeted mouldings may be mounted in this manner by using a crosspiece, as shown below, where the crosspiece is screwed first to the block or blocks and the framed picture is then fastened to the crosspiece. The screw eyes for fastening the frame to the crosspiece are best put on the crosspiece before fastening this to the block. This floating type mount is not readily applicable to works framed under glass.

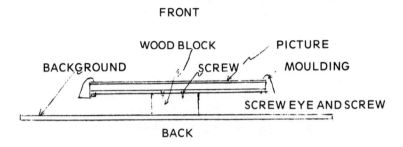

The flat-mount system, since the moulding is screwed to the background, works equally for oils or for works under glass. Work under glass should have the dust cover put on before mounting as the back against the fabric should still have the maximum protection against atmospheric pollutants and deterioration.

This flat-mount system, especially when narrow-legged mouldings are used, may prove a bit difficult for the novice. It is not really difficult, however, and an example may serve to eradicate much of the difficulty.

Refer to the next drawing. This shows the back of such a cloth-covered background plus the framed work to be mounted. In cutting the background originally, the following measurements might have been made, and **do not forget** that the pertinent measurements for this will be made from the **outside edges of the back of the framed work**. Drawing A shows the back of the work. The sight measurement at the front no longer concerns us. Let us assume that it was made for a rabbet measure of 16 x 20 inches. The outside edges of the moulding, however, measure 18 x 22 inches, as indicated. We want 5 inches of background showing all around, or 10 inches added to each dimension. The background board will measure 28 x 32 inches. It will be a bit more after the covering is put on, but this will not be considered in the discussion

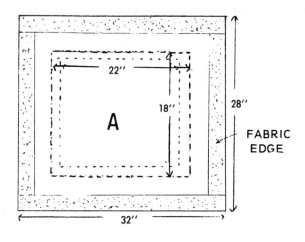

22″

18″

28″

32″

A

FABRIC
EDGE

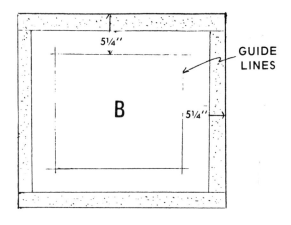

5¼″

5¼″

B

GUIDE
LINES

BACK VIEWS

although it **must** be taken into account in practice. The leg of the moulding is 1 inch wide.

Since we want the screws to be well placed in the moulding, we measure in from each edge of the background 5¼ **inches.** The 5 inches would give us the outside edge of the frame, the extra quarter inch will mark a good position for the screws. Take the T-square or straightedge and make the lines on the **back** of the background board, as shown in diagram B above. Now place the frame on this, face up, to make sure the measurements were correct enough so that none of the lines are outside the frame.

Turn the background board over, letting some 8 inches extend over the table edge, and center the framed work on it in the correct face-up position, as shown in diagram A below. Now measure again to make certain that all sides of the frame are equidistant from the corresponding outer edge of the

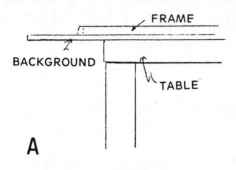

A

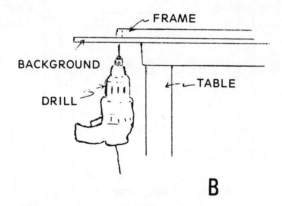

B

background. With the drill in hand, hold the tip of the drill bit on the pencil line visible on the underside of the background, approximately as in B above. Then by viewing with **one** eye, easily determine if the intended hole for the screw will be into the moulding leg or too close to the outside or inside edge of it. If it appears that the tip of the drill is not near enough to the center of the moulding leg, it is easy to shift it the necessary amount without changing position of the eye. Bore this hole, holding the frame steady on the background and then put in the appropriate size screw. Turn the assembly around on the table so that the opposite side is now extending over the edge of the table. Because of possible shifting, align the frame on the backing again to make certain that it is squared. It will not have shifted much, if any, because of the one screw already in. Repeat the process as with the first side, fastening the second side of the frame to the background. Now there can be no shifting and less care is needed. In turn, put screws into the third and fourth sides, so that the back of the finished product is as shown below.

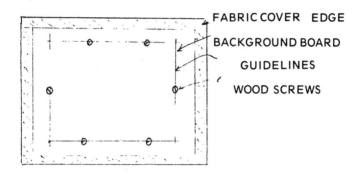

FABRIC COVER EDGE

BACKGROUND BOARD

GUIDELINES

WOOD SCREWS

If plywood is used, measure down and in, equally on both sides, so that the ends of the screw eyes will be inside the capping frame, and put on screw eyes and wire. If Masonite or some other type board was used (which might be too thin to properly hold the screw eyes), the measurements must be carefully made so that the screw eyes will pass through the backboard and **into the capping moulding.** If this is not done, the screw eyes will pull out of the backing.

Earlier it was mentioned that Masonite or similar thin boards could be used better for large sizes if they were "cradled." This is merely a system of bracing from the back and is usually accomplished by use of ⅝ inch furring strips, as shown on the next page. Such cradling adds depth to the background and as a result is not often wanted nor can it be easily adapted to fabric-covered background. These furring strips around the edge can be painted when sanded and finished.

155

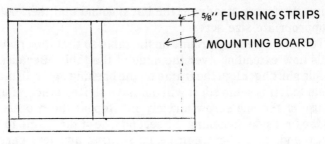

BACK VIEW OF CRADLED MOUNTING

A variation of the mounting to a background may be achieved by adding yet another capping to the edge of the background. Two types are shown below in cross section but these by no means exhaust the possibilities. The first type (A) has obvious advantages in covering cradled Masonite and other boards, though both types are excellent for providing protection to the background's edges. The best choice if such

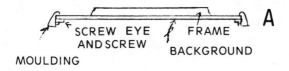

TWO WAYS TO CAP BACKGROUNDS

an additional moulding is used is a simple type capping as indicated above. In either case, it is recommended that the capping be fastened to plywood backgrounds with screw eyes and screws, the same with cradled Masonite or similar boards. If this is not practicable or if a thin background material is used which will not take screw eyes, tack the background in with brads and then strengthen the outer moulding with one or two crossbraces. A sufficiently heavy outer moulding will permit the use of screw eyes and wire for hanging in the outer moulding rather than through the background board.

A very attractive method of mounting old posters, reproductions of ikons, and similar items, is to take a piece of pine (or other) planking and cut a piece just slightly smaller than the item to be mounted, smaller by perhaps ¼ inch. Sand this down very well on the surface and stain the sides and back. Cover the surface with spray adhesive or glue, though for this the spray adhesive is best, and roll the paper print carefully on. Then take the sanding block which was used in removing the excess paper of the dust covers and remove the excess of this paper. With the ball of a ballpeen hammer or any rounded object, hit the surface to create dents, taking care not to tear into or scratch the paper. Any implement which will create such a roughened effect without damage may be used. When this has been done, take the round wood gouge and cut irregular gouges out of the edges in several places, finishing them down with fine sandpaper. The round fine rasps may also be used for this. The diagram below shows the approximate angle of cut. Now run a marking crayon or a bit of

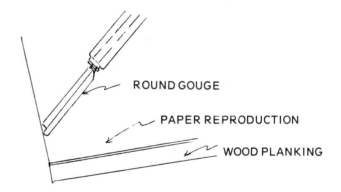

ROUND GOUGE

PAPER REPRODUCTION

WOOD PLANKING

cloth dipped lightly into stain along the edge of the paper to color the white mark showing. When this is dry, put several coats of shellac or plastic from a spray can over the picture area for protection and add a sawtooth hanger on the back. The finished effect is quite "antique" and pleasing. These make excellent groupings.

It is necessary at this point to caution the nonprofessional about mounting his own work either by drymounting or wetmounting. Drymounting, a process of bonding two surfaces together by means of a **mounting tissue** (a thin tissue with shellac base), requires even heat and pressure for successful bonding. There are mounting presses for this work. The nonprofessional may use this system with a common flatiron, instead of the press, on sizes up to 8 x 10 inches or perhaps 11 x 14 inches, but not larger sizes. Even on small items, flatiron often gives unsatisfactory results.

Wetmounting, the use of glues or wheat paste or any other aqueous solution, is also best left in the hands of the professional. The process, which consists merely of coating the back of the item to be mounted and the front surface of the mounting board and then rolling the item down onto the board, tends to produce bubbles and wrinkles which often ruin the work. The item to be mounted, if a type of paper, is soaked by the solution and tends to tear exceedingly easily. Again, this system may be attempted by the beginner only on small items and, until experience is gained, on nothing of value. The other adhesives available, such as contact cement and rubber cement, are not recommended for the beginning framer or for fine art mounting.

An intriguing method of framing for less formal works, especially the outdoor genre of hunting and seascapes, is the "open" or suspended frame. This consists of the framed inner work held in an outer framework by interlaced cords as shown in A and B. The method is simple though it requires care in the execution. The essential need is to have the outer frame exact

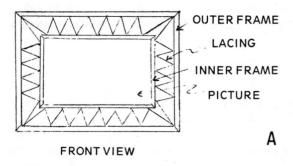

OUTER FRAME
LACING
INNER FRAME
PICTURE

FRONT VIEW

A

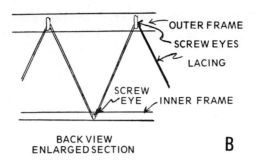

OUTER FRAME
SCREW EYES
LACING
SCREW EYE
INNER FRAME

BACK VIEW
ENLARGED SECTION

B

and squared, and it is well to brace the corners so tension of the laced cord will not pull the outer framework out of square. A sturdy moulding should be selected for both inner frame and outer.

Small screw eyes are placed at intervals not exceeding 2 inches with care that there will be one as near as possible to the corner miter on the outer frame but not on the inner. This is indicated in the diagram. Then a cord is tied to one of the screw eyes (it doesn't matter which one), and laced back and forth in a seesaw effect first to one frame and then to the other until the cord has been passed through all the eyes. When the point of beginning is reached, the end of the cord is secured and the frame is ready for hanging. In the lacing, the cord should be pulled taut periodically, with the two frames in proper relationship so that there will be no shifting when the work is finished. The wall on which the framed work is hung will be visible through the lacings.

If it is easier for the framer, a temporary crosspiece may be tacked across both mouldings so that the work will be held steady and then the cord may be drawn taut as the lacing progresses without pulling the inner frame out of its proper position. This is shown below in the simplified diagram. When the work is finished, this crossbrace is removed.

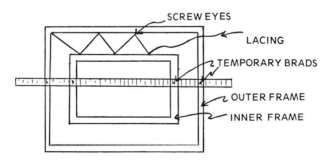

SCREW EYES
LACING
TEMPORARY BRADS
OUTER FRAME
INNER FRAME

Another innovation that we developed which has been used with gratifying results is the **flying frame** shown in face or front view in two designs below. There are obviously many possibilities for variations on this theme. The flying frame consists of the regular framed work supported on an open type brace of finished wood and may be almost flat against the wall or quite far out depending on the intended effect.

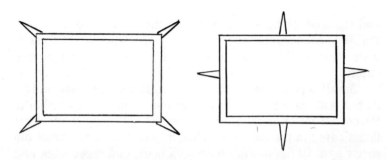

One type of flying frame, the corner radial, is illustrated below in detail showing (A) a side view of one cross leg, followed by (B), a top view of the two cross legs assembled with dotted lines to indicate the position of the framed work.

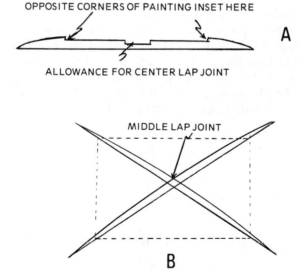

OPPOSITE CORNERS OF PAINTING INSET HERE

A

ALLOWANCE FOR CENTER LAP JOINT

MIDDLE LAP JOINT

B

The illustration on the previous page is a curved crossleg, not easy for the nonprofessional or quite skilled amateur to make. Approximately the same effect may be achieved by using straight strips for the crosslegs, as shown below, with blocks fastened on the back of the legs to hold the crosslegs out from the wall. The ends of the legs in all cases may be finished in ways limited only by your imagination, the squared or the tapered being the easiest to achieve.

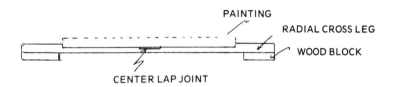

PAINTING

RADIAL CROSS LEG

WOOD BLOCK

CENTER LAP JOINT

Due to a number of factors, including decorator and client demand as well as the inertia of most framers, the processes and quality of framing have remained static if not stagnant for many years. As is historically indicated in many fields and crafts, the professional is bound by his need to make a living from his work and must go with the demand, and few are inclined to try innovations. It is the amateur, the one doing it for love of the work as the origin of the word indicates, who will be more concerned with imaginative application of the principles, as failure is as exciting to him as success. Nor is he concerned only with the aspects of getting the work done in a professional but pedestrian manner. This book has been prepared largely with the nonprofessional framer in mind. Many of these will be hobbyists and many more will be artists, all of a creative tendency. It is our hope that you have been stimulated to trying something new!

INDEX

INDEX